Pulpit Speech

JAY E. ADAMS

BAKER BOOK HOUSE
Grand Rapids, Michigan

ISBN: 0-8010-0106-4

First printing, May 1976
Second printing, February 1979

PHOTOLITHOPRINTED BY CUSHING - MALLOY, INC.
ANN ARBOR, MICHIGAN, UNITED STATES OF AMERICA
1979

PREFACE

This book is intended for three classes of persons:

1. Ministers in the pastorate who wish to brush up on their pulpit speech. Many were trained ineffectively and need the sort of practical help that this book seeks to offer.

2. Students in preministerial courses in Christian colleges or Bible schools.

3. Seminary students in a pre-preaching speech course.

The textbook format includes suggested classroom projects at the conclusion of the chapters, and has been adopted as providing the most complete form. Ministers will note that many of the assignments also may be done on a do-it-yourself basis. It is my hope in publishing this volume that it will provide practical guidance for those who must preach the Word, and thus will contribute in some small way to the revival of the proclamation of the truth in our time.

Jay Adams
Philadelphia, 1971

CONTENTS

FIGURES AND ILLUSTRATIONS

INTRODUCTION

Clyde Reid, in his book *The Empty Pulpit*, contends that preaching is passé. A homiletics professor at one famous liberal seminary claims that no one comes to chapel to hear a preacher or speaker any more: "You can only get them out to hear a Combo," he said. Another professor of preaching said that of 113 entering juniors, only six elected the course in preaching (at his seminary, all preaching courses are elective). This man maintains that he lured the six by offering a course in *experimental* preaching in which the students may show slides, give nonverbal sermons, etc. Preaching as such is not even required. The word is abroad that preaching has had it.

This idea has not been contested strongly by conservative Christians.[1] Indeed, here and there one hears conservatives saying much the same thing. A professor of homiletics at a seminary with a conservative reputation recently said that he believes that in the near future drama will replace preaching. Others believe preaching has a place, yet see little hope for it, and are terribly dismayed. Preaching, it would seem, has fallen upon hard times.

Ours, then, does not seem to be a very appropriate season for preaching. However, we must not forget that God knew that there would be times when preaching would be looked upon unfavorably. And so to encourage Timothy, the Spirit moved the apostle to write: "Preach the word; be ready in season and out of season" (II Tim. 4:2). The word to Timothy is a prophetic word to us as well. Paul insists that the Christian minister must preach the word in all seasons, not only when the times are favorable. Whether our times are

---

[1] One virile defense was made by Leonard Verduin, who cogently contends that the abandonment of preaching has theological roots. He sees the acceptance of event-revelation rather than word-revelation at the bottom of the problem. "No More Sermons?" *The Banner*, December 19, 1969; December 26, 1969.

eukairos (favorable times) for preaching or *akairos* (unfavorable times) really has no bearing upon the question. A preacher of Jesus Christ must preach in both periods. There is no hedging here. The sentence is an imperative. Moreover, it is part of a solemn charge given by Paul to Timothy as a minister of the Word of God (vs. 1). The introductory word *be ready (ephistemi)* means *stand by,* or "be at hand." The command is not to stop preaching, but to continue preaching. Paul anticipated bad times for preaching, yet he charged faithful ministers to "stay by" their preaching posts. The minister, then, must preach even in *akairos* times. So if our day is *akairos,* we must face the fact realistically, but may not cease preaching.

But, of course, we must be careful not to brand the times as unfavorable if the disenchantment with preaching is the fault of preachers rather than a problem of the times. There is good reason to think that poor preaching is at the base of many (if not most) of the complaints about the pulpit heard today. A minister must not too quickly throw off on his times that for which he should blame only himself. Good preaching is getting an enthusiastic hearing in a number of places today. It is well, then, to ask the question, is our day truly *akairos?* It may be much too early to say. It would seem presumptuous to claim that preaching is all but ready to disappear.

The rapidly changing events of the last ten years have sent people out into the streets demonstrating, and on each of these occasions demonstrators have proclaimed their message by word of mouth; not always effectively, but not always ineffectively, either. Ten to fifteen years ago who could have predicted that such a spate of public speaking was about to become fashionable? Just a few years ago in one of my messages I recall appealing to men in the Orthodox Presbyterian Church to enter the ministry since the need was so great. At the time of writing this Introduction, the latest figure of which I have any knowledge shows fifty men under care of presbytery, with very few pulpits open and available. What a tremendous change! Perhaps the work that God has been doing in the smaller denominations that are true to the Scriptures is now about to make an impact upon our nation. If so, the movement will both bring about a great revival of the right kind of preaching and also will be brought about by such preaching. Conservative seminaries are growing, while the student bodies of liberal seminaries are diminishing. Smaller conservative denominations are coming to the front. God may very well have a new era ahead for the Church in this land. Why has he prepared such organizations? Why are conservative seminaries blooming? Is there a great work ahead? What will happen to the liberal congregations when there are no preachers available? Will these churches dry up on the vine or will they be forced to turn to conservative seminaries for preachers? If so, if revival comes, if there is a great day coming for the Church of Christ and for the country, you may be sure of one thing: it will be a revival sparked by preaching. This has been true of all past revivals of the Christian faith. They have all directly involved the faithful preaching of the Word, the preaching of the Christ who saves. The next ten to fifteen years may hold the answer. That is one reason why conservatives must faithfully study the art of preaching.

Today is a day of rapid transition; we do not know yet what the new age will be like. The new age will be *eukairos* or *akairos* for preaching. Whatever the final verdict, the answer for the conservative preacher will be the same: he must preach the Word in season or out of season. And where that Word is preached, men (many or few) will be saved and grow in grace. Since he must "stand by" and never abandon preaching, the conservative always will be deeply concerned with speech, for this is the primary medium by which he proclaims the message of life.

This course in the elements of pulpit speech has been designed primarily as a pre-preaching course. It presupposes that at length the student will study the principles and practice of homiletics, and, therefore, makes no attempt to deal with homiletics as such. Yet the speech needs of the *minister* have been kept in the forefront at all times. Hopefully, pastors too may benefit from using this book as a refresher course.

Lucid speech is not a natural gift. The privileged few were born into a family or raised in a community where, from the earliest years, they heard and imitated good speech. For most of us, however, such speech must be attained (if indeed it is attained at all) at great cost. But in either case the point of importance is that *lucid speech is learned behavior.*

Just as we learned to speak English, Spanish, or Hindustani by imitating the language of our parents and peers, so too, our pronunciation, style and even most aspects of our delivery (the use of voice and body) are learned in a similar fashion. Unfortunately, therefore, many of our earliest habits of speech must be unlearned.

One study indicated that the average person spends nine per cent of his waking hours writing, sixteen per cent reading, thirty per cent speaking, and forty-five per cent listening.[2] Yet, throughout the early years of elementary and grade schools in America, nearly all of the effort expended on communication is directed toward assuring excellence in reading and writing, while speech and listening are almost totally ignored.[3] Since a child comes to school already speaking, it is frequently (though wrongly) assumed that this skill has been

---

[2] Paul T. Rankin, "Listening Ability," *Chicago Schools Journal,* January 1930, pp. 177-179. James H. McBurney says, "The average person necessarily speaks ten to twenty times as much as he writes . . ." The University of Missouri *Bulletin,* Vol. 55, No. 1, 1954, p. 24.

[3] This is a modern phenomenon. All antiquity recognized the vital importance of training in speech. Greek and Roman schools were the most famous for their instruction in public speaking, but we possess also manuscripts from Egypt going back to a period before Cheops that indicate an interest in speech education. Throughout the early days of European history, speech (rhetoric) was one of the three courses in the educational *trivium* (logic and grammar, closely related subjects, were the others). Modern American reluctance to teach public speaking stems largely from reactions to the elocutionary movement.

mastered already. Unfortunately, therefore, little or no attention is given to instruction in speech in the grammar schools. Time is devoted to acquiring skill in reading and writing (new skills), but speech is neglected. Often poor speech patterns develop and harden with little or no concern on the part of teachers. And most teachers would not have the competence to help if they cared to do so. Now, at this late date, in college or seminary, something needs to be done. It is possible that such relearning may at first seem very difficult, since you will not merely be learning new speech skills, but in some instances also breaking long-standing patterns. Because of this fact, you will be wise to give careful daily attention to your assignments.

Though you may experience some early difficulty with the assignments in this course, you will probably discover (usually somewhere around the time you give your second or third speech) that few courses in a college or theological curriculum can be as enjoyable as this one. Many of you may be new at the seminary and may not yet know one another very well. But by the end of the course you probably will be surprised at how well you have come to know each other. This course, I think you will pleasantly discover, affords a unique opportunity for you to come to know your fellow students. For it is here that both they and you will begin to give voice to your ideas, prejudices, errors, feelings, questions, attitudes, and convictions. But remember, too, that it is your responsibility to make the course interesting and enjoyable. In a very real sense this is your course. You will produce most of its classroom content. Unlike most other classes, in this course you and your classmates will be standing at the front of the room. It is your course in every sense of the word. Therefore, by the effort or lack of effort that you put into it, you will determine how valuable and how interesting the course will be. I hope that because it is your own you will determine to make it a fine course, one of your very best.

Chapter One

SPEECH ARTS AND FACTORS
IN THE PREACHING SITUATION

In this chapter we shall roam over the whole territory of pulpit speech in order to compile some initial rough generalizations. Perhaps we should ask first of all, What is speech? One way of answering that question is to say that good speech is the oral communication of true and worthwhile content, well organized, delivered effectively in clear and appropriate language that achieves desired ends. All of these elements are involved in pulpit speech, but there is more.[1] In order to discover some of these additional elements, let us look immediately at the preaching situation.

THE PREACHING SITUATION

The preaching situation involves four arts governed by four factors. Another way to say this is to speak of each of the four arts viewed in four aspects. Or perhaps we might say, preaching requires skill in four arts performed in four dimensions (or contexts). Whatever the best approach may be, the preacher must recognize that there are eight elements involved in the preaching situation. About each of these he needs to be well informed.

The four arts are: the art of researching content, the art of organization, the art of language usage, and the art of delivery. These four arts may be summed up by the mnemonic device C-O-L-D. The four factors with which they interact are

---

[1]The difference between pulpit speech and other forms of speech for the Christian does not lie in the fact that the one is a sacred language or speech about sacred subjects. All language and all subjects are sacred to the Christian who sees God as the author of all things, including speech. Pulpit speech involves the authoritative proclamation by word of the written Word and its redemptive message concerning Jesus Christ, who is the living Word.

the Scriptures, the occasion, the audience, and the preacher. These may be conveniently remembered by the word S-O-A-P. These four arts and factors can readily be recalled by simply remembering the two words COLD SOAP.

All eight of these elements are interrelated and overlap so that it is difficult to represent their relationships in a single schematic diagram. We shall return to each of them after a while and throughout this course, but for now take a look at the following chart:

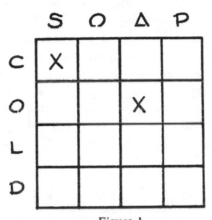

Figure 1
Heterogeneous Grid showing the relation-
ships between the eight elements in the
Preaching Situation.

In the chart (Figure 1) you see a heterogeneous grid. Across the top is the word SOAP (standing for Scripture, Occasion, Audience and Preacher). Running down the left-hand margin is the word COLD (standing for Content, Organization, Language and Delivery). You will notice an X in the box where the column labeled "Scripture" intersects the line labeled "Content." This indicates that the Scriptures as one factor in the preaching situation have a direct relationship to the total content of the sermon. The study of this relationship is essential. Here such matters as exegesis, the general and specific purpose, and the use of supplemental materials must be discussed. In all there are 16 combinations: SC, SO, SL, SD, OC, etc. Take another example. You notice that if you run vertically down the A (or Audience) column, it will overlap the O line (Organization) at the third block across (note the X), bringing audience and organization into contact with one another. This interaction raises such questions as, "What kind of sermon organization is best to use with what sort of audience?" If the audience is hostile, how does that affect organization; if the audience is friendly, how does that affect organization? And so, it is possible (and essential) to discuss the interrelationships that develop in each block of this heterogeneous grid.[2] There are relationships (often unrecognized) between the four arts and the four factors in every sermon. But the preaching situation is still more complex. Two other grids are necessary to show the further significant relationships that exist. For example, the following grid (Figure 2) is a homogeneous grid in which COLD runs across the top and also down the side. Figure 3 is another homogeneous grid in

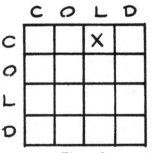

Figure 2
Homogeneous Grid showing interrelationships of the Four Arts.

_____

[2]The student will find it profitable to think through each block for himself and make a list of as many questions as are raised by the intersection of the four arts and factors. The same procedure would be useful also in understanding the material that follows.

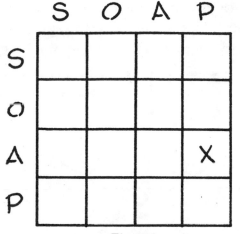

Figure 3
Homogeneous grid showing interrelationships of the Four Factors.

which SOAP appears both across the top and down the side. These grids indicate that in addition to the interaction between the Arts and the Factors in the preaching situation, there is also interaction between the Arts themselves and the Factors themselves. How is it that these interract? It should not be difficult to see that there are key places where interaction occurs. For example, in Figure 3 the vital relationship of the preacher (represented by the P column) to the audience (represented by the A line) ought to be obvious. Here such matters as the conjunction of the personality and ecclesiastical affiliation of the preacher and the doctrinal set and attitude of the audience raise a host of interesting questions. In the first homogeneous grid (Figure 2) you can easily see how language (the L column) and content (the C line) need to be related. The rest of the possible relationships also ought to be considered. Students may be assigned reports on each of the blocks in the grids. Perhaps in this summary fashion, however, you can begin to see something of the complexity of the preaching situation and the problems that are involved in it.

ABSTRACTING THE PURPOSE

You will notice in the following diagram (Figure 4) that there are really two areas in which the speaker must work.

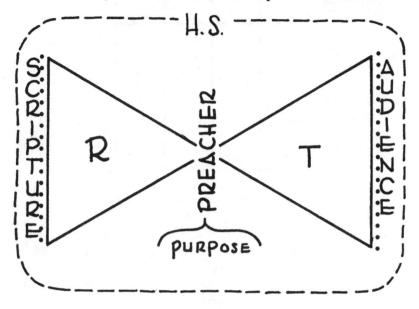

Figure 4
The Two Areas and the Purpose

The triangle R represents research skills and the triangle T represents transmission skills. Down the left side next to a line of dots is the word Scripture. To the right of the diagram is another series of dots labeled Audience. Each series of dots represents a group of particulars. The first group of particulars is comprised of specific data from the Scriptures that have to be researched, which must be systematically related to one another and toward which the preacher must direct historical, grammatical, biblical-theological exegesis and interpretation. In other words, before he can deliver the goods the preacher must get the goods. On the other side of the diagram is another group of particulars representing the specific knowledge, needs and attitudes of concrete individuals, together with all of the differences of age, background, culture, etc. These also must be studied and understood so that the particulars of the Scriptures may be brought cogently to bear upon the particulars of the congregation. Where the two triangles meet is the preacher. His work, on the one hand, is to do research in the Scriptures in order to gather the facts, determine the purpose, organize the material, and to summarize all of this in terms of a particular principle which expresses the intention of the Holy Spirit in putting this passage into permanent scriptural form. His task is to determine what the Holy Spirit wants this passage to do for his congregation. This purpose may be stated as a principle or theme around which the sermon is organized psychologically, the language (style) is developed, and the delivery and specific applications take shape. In this form the passage is brought to the particular members of the congregation. Here transmission skill (or delivering the goods) is required. In the process of preparation and preaching there is movement from the particular to the general and then back to the particular. All of this is done in the context of the Holy Spirit (indicated by the dotted line encircling the whole figure). Much more needs to be said about these two aspects of the preacher's work.

One thing more may be said here: most of what you will learn in this course is involved with the second triangle, which has to do largely with transmission skills. We will be concerned more about delivering the goods than about getting the goods. However, since the diagram clearly shows the importance of both of these matters, we cannot stress strongly enough the need for good research skills. Hopefully, in other departments of the seminary and from past training, some ways and means for researching will have been acquired and will continue to be developed. The particular emphasis of this course, however, which must assume the existence of research skills (rightly or wrongly), is upon the second triangle.

CONTENT AND PURPOSE

When you think about content, you must think about at least three things: first, the subject area or over-all theme; second, the purpose (in preaching this means God's purpose, i.e., the Holy Spirit's purpose in including the passage in the Scriptures); third, other supplemental materials.

While this is not the place to discuss the preacher's purpose *(telos)* in detail, perhaps a word here may be appropriate.[3] Each sermon has a general and specific purpose, a telic dimension that involves a *telos* toward which, out of which and around which all of the sermon moves. The word *telos* means, "the goal, purpose, end or aim." The telic note should dominate the message. The *telos* determines the preaching portion. The *telos* of a sermon may be large or small, it may contain sub-*teloi* or may be one of several such sub-*teloi*. It should be the unifying factor in every sermon, without exception.

To discover the Holy Spirit's *telos* is the reason for our exegetical work. Some people seem to think that exegesis exists in a vacuum for itself. But exegesis is incomplete without the telic note. The culmination of exegesis is to discover the Holy Spirit's purpose in including the preaching portion in the canon. We are concerned about discovering the purpose for which the passage was given by the Holy Spirit so that we may use it for the proper purpose for which it was intended to help our listeners. When we discover the Holy Spirit's *telos,* and use the preaching portion for that purpose, we will use that portion of the Scriptures *as God intended it* to be used. Other uses are misuses.

DETERMINING THE MATERIALS TO BE USED

An old Puritan recipe for cooking turkey began, "First catch your turkey." Obviously, research comes first. This is

---

[3]Strictly speaking this matter should be reserved for homiletics. It is my plan to discuss this matter fully in a forthcoming book on homiletics.

the only way to get the preaching materials in hand. There are various types of preaching materials which must be distinguished. These are factual, logical, psychological, and illustrative.

The *factual materials* consist fundamentally of two sorts:

1. *Basic materials.* These materials consist of the infallible revelational words of God in the Scriptures. Here there can be no error except in the preacher's interpretation of the basic materials. The materials, themselves, are, in the original languages, perfect and true.

2. *Supplemental materials.* These materials consist of historical, biographical, statistical, archeological, and many other kinds of information that may be brought into a sermon to supplement the basic biblical materials. But their function is clearly supplemental. Basically, a sermon preaches Christ as he is found in the passage of Scripture at hand.[4] Supplemental materials raise not only the problem of interpretation, but also the problem of error in the materials themselves.

Logical materials consist of those kinds of materials that are used in argumentation that enable one to reason from the biblical facts (as interpreted by the preacher) to conclusions and applications pertaining to the audience. This argumentation may involve argument from analogy, from cause to effect, effect to cause, etc.[5]

Psychological materials consist of those sorts of materials that evoke an affective response from the listener. They are

---

[4]Christ is the subject of all the Scriptures: cf. Luke 24:27. The Scriptures are "opened" (explained properly—vss. 27, 32) when Christ is seen in "all the Scriptures." It is then that hearts are set on fire (vs. 32). Cf. E. P. Clowney, *Preaching and Biblical Theology,* Grand Rapids: Eerdmans, 1961.

[5]A study of the book of Galatians reveals the fact that Paul used a number of different sorts of arguments in contending for justification by faith alone. In chapters 3-5, as many as eight or nine types of argumentation have been distinguished.

motivational materials, and as such consist of emotionally charged words, stories, and phrases.

Illustrative materials comprise such things as examples, instances (shortened examples), figures of speech, and imagery. These serve to clarify, impress, concretize and make the other materials relevant.

PURPOSE AND MATERIALS

The materials and methods that one uses are closely related to and should be determined by the biblical purpose. This is one of the crucial reasons why the preacher's purpose in each sermon must be clear. Without such clarity it is impossible to know the type of materials to use at any given point or throughout a message.

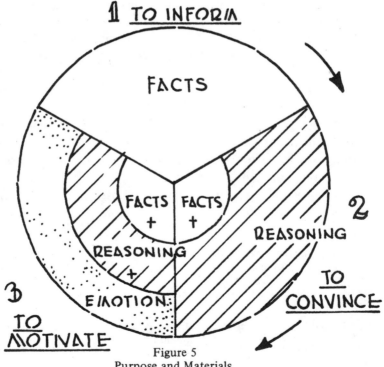

Figure 5
Purpose and Materials

SOURCES OF SUPPLEMENTAL MATERIALS

Supplemental materials may be obtained in more ways than can be mentioned here. However, a few suggestions may be useful to the beginning student.

1. *Borrowing* All of us borrow. A study of the biblical use of the word "imitation" *(mimeo)* and *tupos* (type, pattern, model) shows that God expects each of us to imitate others; that much is assumed, not even questioned.[6] The only questions are how to imitate, what to imitate, and whom to imitate. The important matter here, however, is the ethics of borrowing. There are fundamentally only two ways to borrow: one may borrow directly or indirectly. Direct borrowing obligates the borrower to credit the source from which the material was obtained. Indirect borrowing, however, is a different matter. A suggestion by Oliver Wendell Holmes at this point pretty well points to the best solution to the problem. Holmes said, "I have milked 300 cows, but I made my own butter."[7] This direct borrowing from Holmes (in which I credit him) speaks of indirect borrowing. He clearly tells us that there is something that each individual can bring to old material: new organization, new integration with other materials, etc. Someone asked Sir Joshua Reynolds how long it took him to paint a certain picture. His answer was, "All my life." The preacher must learn how to churn materials through his own mind so as to make them truly his own. He must bring the thoughts of others into a new relationship with the Scriptures, into relationship with his own experience, and into relationship with the particular congregation to whom he is speaking. Sermons which are nothing more than one week's study are almost invariably not the preacher's own. There must be a

---

[6]Cf. Jay Adams, *Competent to Counsel*, Philadelphia: Presbyterian and Reformed Publishing Company, pp. 177 ff.

[7]Quoted by A. W. Blackwood, *Pulpit Digest*, XXXIII, January 1953, p. 16.

part of every preacher himself in every sermon he preaches. The new syntheses of materials, that includes indirect borrowing, are perhaps the best supplemental materials.

2. *One's own experiences.* Turning to your own experience is a very good way to begin whenever you want to obtain supplementary materials. Usually such materials can be described more powerfully with more detail and vividness because you were there. Experience brings a certain authenticity to what one says; it lends a relevant contemporaneity to the sermon and usually evokes a sympathetic response. A message illustrated by that common fund of human problems of which Paul wrote in I Corinthians 10:1-13[8] sets heads to nodding as members of the congregation recognize that the preacher is bowling down their alley.

When you draw from the fund of your own experience you may turn to your own particular interests and specialties, i.e., to areas in which you already possess some competence. It is foolish, therefore, for the preacher to neglect the personal storehouse of information that he has been accumulating throughout his life.

3. *Occasions near at hand.* It is often wise to acknowledge those events and occasions that are of importance to the listener. One excellent way to do this is through the judicious use of occasional supplemental content. When elections are at hand, it is the third of July, or school will begin in one more week, a preacher does well to refer to such matters. This does not mean that he must preach a sermon directed toward these events; usually he will not want to do so. But his supplementary materials may be drawn from the occasion or applied to it with power and profit. The members of the congregation are already oriented toward such occasions and events and a fair amount of their time and discussion may be taken up with these matters. Ask: "How does the event illustrate some

---

[8]Adams, *op. cit.,* pp. 58, 90, 131 ff., 254.

point in the message?" Ask: "Does this message in some way bear upon the way my congregation should think or act on this occasion?" Such contemporary preaching often brings home with clarity truths otherwise difficult to understand.

4. *Conversation and personal contact.* Not only may casual conversation be the source of valuable supplementary materials, but planned contact with people may also elicit useful information. Indeed, one may even rely at times upon personal interviews, surveys or polls. Visitation and pastoral counseling provide a prime source for supplemental material. But it is important for the preacher always to do the hard work of carefully flattening out all such materials before they are used publicly in sermons. Unless he has agreed to allow you to use such information without emendation, a member of the congregation must not be able to recognize references to himself in your sermons. Preachers at times have destroyed their own effectiveness as pastoral counselors by divulging material and embarrassing people publicly. It is also important for each member of the congregation to know that the flattening out process has taken place so that he may be sure that if he were to come to the pastor with a problem of his own, the private information he revealed would not be used in recognizable form in preaching in this or in some later pastorate.

BEGINNING TO GATHER MATERIALS

It would be wise to begin (right now) to collect illustrative materials. Christ and his apostles constantly translated the cosmos into the language of faith. Jesus used flowers, doors, sheep, water, bread, roads, trees, etc. to teach truth understandably and vividly. The preacher must also learn to do the same. One way to begin to "see" illustrations of truth wherever you turn is to discipline yourself to do so. You may determine to discover at least five simple illustrations every day for three months, using only objects in your room or study.

Write down and revise these daily. Perhaps you will also begin to write illustrative material in several books that have numbered pages, which you might entitle:

Things Seen - Things Heard - Things Read - Things Thought

Each of these might be labeled topically or textually and filed in your 3 x 5 universal file accordingly.

SUGGESTED PROJECTS
For Classroom or Study

In the Classroom

1. Choose one block from each of the grids (COLD/SOAP, COLD/COLD, SOAP/SOAP) and write a 1-2 page report to be read to the class, discussing the interaction of the factors and arts involved. (This paper need not be handed in.)

2. Examine your interests and resources and list nine possible topics (not sermons, but probably with content that might be used in a sermon) about which you might speak during the coming weeks.

Topics

A. To Inform

_____

_____

_____

B. To Convince

_____

_____

_____

C. To Motivate

_____

_____

_____

3. Hand in a two-page audience analysis consisting of the following:

Page One: A summary of significant data concerning the members of the group to whom you will speak.

Page Two: A choice of one topic from each of the three categories listed above with a full explanation of why you have chosen these three topics in the light of your resources and the audience analysis.

In the Study

1. Work through the interaction of factors and arts in each grid. Make a list of possible implications. Keep this list handy when preparing sermons.
2. Make an audience analysis of your congregation. Refer to this analysis when preparing future sermons.

Chapter Two

THE USE OF NARRATIVE IN PREACHING
(The Preacher as a Storyteller)

A narrative is a story. Everyone from his first childhood well into his second enjoys a story. Picture an all-too-typical classroom scene: a dry lecture is being delivered by a teacher who has lost his class. Half of the students are nearly asleep, the other half are perfunctorily taking notes. The speaker says, "Let me tell you a personal experience that illustrates this point." Heads pop up and the class magically awakens. Why? Because the teacher is about to tell a story.

Narrative speaking figured largely in Christ's preaching. Again and again the New Testament represents Christ telling stories. Christ knew the values of the narrative method and capitalized on them; every preacher must learn to do the same. The parable, one of Christ's chief teaching forms, is a narrative form. No wonder, then, that the common people heard him gladly.

We shall begin with the narrative for three reasons. First, the narrative is the easiest speech with which to begin. It is easy to tell a story because of its inherent interest value; most people readily respond to narratives. A good narrative is also easier to construct and to tell than other kinds of speeches. Second, narrative speaking logically precedes the other types of pulpit speaking that we must consider. We shall proceed from the simple to the more complex. Each new type of speech will demand new elements *in combination with* (not in place of) the former type of speech. That means, the narrative may be used in conjunction with other forms of speech. Usually when it is so used it is called an illustration or example. Third, the narrative demands the fullest use of delivery from the outset, forcing the student to consider this important aspect of speech immediately. Unless he does so, he may continue or develop poor patterns of delivery during the early part of the course that will have to be unlearned later on.

CHOICE AND LIMITATION OF SUBJECT MATTER

Fundamentally there are just two kinds of narratives: the real and the fictitious. The real may come either from your own personal experience, or from the experience of someone else. For the beginner it is better to begin with a real narrative of something that actually happened to you. It is usually much easier to remember and describe a real situation in which you were personally involved than it is to invent not only the plot but also the details of a fictitious one.

Initially the beginner is likely to find it difficult to limit his subject. He recognizes that he must fill a certain amount of time with verbalized information and, therefore, frequently chooses a large topic hoping that it will afford him sufficient material to cover the entire five- or ten-minute period assigned to him. However, he soon is likely to become quite frustrated. Something is wrong; the speech seems dull, uninteresting. Although he usually does not recognize it, the reason for this frustration is that his subject is too broad. He has failed to consider that one can say much more in a small period of time, about a narrower subject, than he can about a larger one. Learning from the laser, he must discover the power of a concentrated beam of light. Large subjects, broad abstract topics, and wide ranging themes can only be outlined or sketched in a brief period of time. The kind of colorful detail and specific concrete material that is necessary to make a narrative vital and to make the subject live, is impossible in broad topics. As a result, such speeches tend to become dull and uninteresting. You can't say very much in two or three minutes (or for that matter in twenty or thirty minutes); so in order to say anything well it is essential to *limit*.

The principle to grasp at all costs is that you can say more about less. For example, a sermon on the subject of "Prophecy" is much too large. You might want to narrow that subject to limit it to one aspect of prophetic study, such as "The Second Coming." And yet, think of the breadth of the second coming as a topic for a sermon. Think about the great controversy there has been over the second coming; think of how many aspects there are to that topic; think about how much information there is in the Scriptures concerning it: someone has said one fourth of the New Testament relates to it. Clearly, then, the subject, "The Second Coming," though an aspect of the broader topic "Prophecy," itself needs to be limited. So let's take one aspect of the topic, "The Second Coming," for example: "Implications of the Second Coming." But even this is much too broad. There are so many implications of the second coming. "All right," you say, "let's limit the implica - tions of the second coming to 'Implications for Believers,' " But still, you know how many implications of the second coming there are for believers. So after all this, you finally decide to narrow your topic to one aspect of the implications of the second coming for believers, namely, one implication: e.g., "Purity" (I John 3:3), or "Comfort" (I Thessalonians 4:13 ff.).

What the preacher needs to learn is that a rifle is much more powerful in preaching than a shotgun. Limitation keeps a preacher from scattering his shot. If he carefully limits his sermon he will not run out of sermon topics during his first or second year in the pastorate. His congregation will not go home confused because he has told them too little about too much. They will go home clearly understanding and deeply concerned about one thing in depth. It would be well for a preacher to imagine that someone has offered to give him $50 for every sermon that he could legitimately preach on an aspect of the subject that he has chosen. Hardly any other problem presents itself more pointedly at the outset than the problem of limitation. That is why the narrative you will give in this course should be limited to one story about one brief event that is complete in itself.

THE BASIC NARRATIVE PLAN

There are, of course, many ways in which narratives can be presented. Some ways are far more sophisticated than others. The flashback method, for example, in which one begins at or near the end of the story and then goes back and unfolds the steps leading toward their ultimate consequences is one variation on the basic theme. But for a beginner, the best way to begin is to let the story unfold as it happened. Instead of jumping into the middle of the action, it is better for a beginner to use the basic narrative plan so that he does not give away the plot or the climax too soon. More sophisticated methods will be possible later when one becomes more adept in the use of the narrative. The following diagram (Figure 6) demonstrates plainly the basic narrative plan with each of the essential elements contained in it.

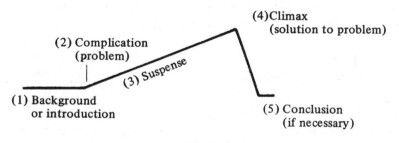

Figure 6
The Basic Narrative Plan

You will note on the diagram above that there are the following elements: (1) background or introductory material; (2) the introduction of a problem or some complication; (3) suspense which builds through new complications, failures to solve the original problem or new insights into the problem; (4) a climax or solution to the problem or problems; and (5) though not absolutely necessary, a very brief conclusion. (Notice how the interest level rises to the climax then drops abruptly.) The climax at times may be identical with the conclusion.

BACKGROUND

Background materials should not always be sketched explicitly; often information may be conveyed incidentally by suggestive hints while saying something else. There is a well known form of Japanese poetry called Haiku, which uses just such a methodology to suggest some season of the year, as well as the point of the poem. Both must be inferred, since neither is stated explicitly. The following sample of Haiku poetry is a wonderful spoof on the stupidity of idolatry. You will doubtless notice also the season which is implied but not stated.

> Oh Buddha on the wall
> From thy holy nose indeed
> There hangs — an icicle.

You will notice, too, the periodic nature of this poetry in which the meaning, purpose and punch are suspended until the very end. Here the climax and meaning of the poem coalesce in the one last word: "icicle."

Background material should consist only of such material as will be of definite value to an understanding of the story. Other interesting but extraneous bits of information only detract and tend to lead the listener down false paths. It is important, then, to sift carefully the background material in a narrative, so that only those elements that are absolutely necessary remain. In telling a story, it is all too easy to get caught up in what a friend has called the "lace curtains." By "lace curtains" she means that when she tells a story she goes into so many extraneous details that it takes forever to get to the point. But it is important to note that some vital details may at first seem extraneous. Such information may be planted in the introductory or background part of the narrative and at that point may seem extraneous, yet it proves to be essential to an understanding of some later point in the narrative. Seeding the introduction with all such information takes care and deliberation. You can see therefore that it is often, if not al-

ways, essential to write (or at least carefully revise) the introduction after the rest of the narrative has been composed. In
the story of the Good Samaritan (Luke 10:25-37), it might at
first seem unimportant to mention the insults and injuries in-
flicted upon the traveler who "fell among thieves." But Christ
notes that they "stripped him, beat him" and "left him half
dead" (vs. 30). Reflection shows that it is vital to know his
condition: (1) so that the enormity of the sin of the priest
and the Levite may be established—they passed by a man in
that shape! and (2) so that the greatness of the love of the
Samaritan may be shown in meeting the man's every need
(vss. 34, 35).

COMPLICATION

The intrusion of a complication or problem into the narrative immediately arouses a certain amount of concern and
curiosity. The complication represents the beginning of the
suspense that hopefully will build to the climax. If you study
Christ's parables, you will find that the introduction of the
problem (or complicating factor) comes early, usually following a minimum of background material. For example, in the
parable of the Pharisee and the Publican (Luke 18:9 ff.) the
complication is introduced in the second sentence:

> "Two men went up into the temple to pray, the one was
> a Pharisee and the other was a Publican" (background ma-
> terial[1]). "The Pharisee prayed thus *with himself* . . ."

Immediately the characterization of the Pharisee's prayer as
prayer "with himself" raises several problems: 1. What do
these words mean? 2. What will be the outcome of the story?
3. What point is Jesus about to make by characterizing prayer
that way? Those opening words of the second sentence raise

---

[1]Even here a certain amount of complication is already present in
the sharp contrast between the Pharisee (the most socially respected
man) and the Publican (the most socially despised man).

questions. And indeed, the questions that they raise demand a solution (climax). A careful study of the parables of Jesus will show that sometimes, however, it is necessary to preface the complicating factor with a larger amount of preliminary information (e.g., note some of the parables in Matthew 13). But ordinarily the problem or complication is introduced quite early. This point cannot be stressed strongly enough. Background material can be interesting but not for long, and certainly not as an end in itself. The most interesting factor in a narrative is not the background but the problem itself. Therefore, it is important to move on to the complication as quickly as possible.

SUSPENSE

The third element in a good narrative is suspense. I noted earlier that suspense grows as the story develops. Growing suspense is generated largely through the introduction of additional complications, failures to solve the problem, new insights into the problem, etc. You see this in the parable that we have begun to consider. Two men, one a Pharisee, the other a Publican, have entered the temple to pray. One prays with himself:

> "I thank thee God that I am not as other men are, extortioners, unjust, adulterers, or even as this Publican. I fast twice in the week, I give tithes of all that I earn."

This additional information helps us to understand what it is that is wrong with the man's prayer; now we begin to understand why Jesus characterized his prayer as prayer "with himself." The problem is that he does not pray at all. He simply boasts; he spends his time telling God how good he is. Jesus implied that such prayers do not go farther than the man who offers them. While answering the first of the three questions (mentioned earlier), this new insight only intensifies the second and third. Next, Christ reinforces the contrast by introducing the humble, efficacious prayer of the Publican. The note of contrast is struck with finesse and simplicity.

"The Publican, standing afar off, would not so much as lift up his eyes unto heaven, but smote upon his breast, saying, God be merciful to me a sinner."

In one sentence, the elements of extreme contrast are brought into juxtaposition as the picture of the two men is completed.

CLIMAX

As suspense is built by the introduction of new and contrasting material that lays bare the severity of the problem, the question that takes shape and with urgency demands an answer is: what is the point, what is it that Jesus wants me to learn? In reply, Jesus succinctly but powerfully resolves the whole matter by conjoining both climax and conclusion:

"I tell you this man (the Publican) went down to his house justified rather than the other, for whoever exalts himself will be abased and whoever abases himself will be exalted."

There was no long working out of a moral, there was no detailed direct application of the story, there was no muddying of the canvas by lingering over the point; no, precisely not that. Indeed, in one pointed pregnant sentence Jesus tied all together, answered all the questions, made the point, and by implication powerfully applied it to his hearers.

It is extremely important to know the climax quite well before beginning to tell the story. In fact, there are times when it is just as crucial to know the exact words in which the climax will be phrased as it is to know the exact words in the punch line of a joke. Every question that is raised in building suspense should be resolved in the climax. Otherwise people will go away asking themselves questions about minor aspects of the presentation that will shift the focus of their attention from the main point.

CONCLUSION

Too frequently speakers feel the necessity to explain the point of the narrative and often go into great detail in doing so. They like to stand off and take a second hard look at what has been said. Whenever this happens it is almost as annoying as explaining the punch line of a joke. As much as possible, let the story speak for itself. If there is something that must be explained, do it quickly and briefly. Frequently the climax and conclusion will coalesce; whenever possible, allow them to do so.

Preachers should take lessons from Jesus himself, the greatest story teller of all time. The professor may wish to assign several of the parables of Jesus Christ to each student for analysis. The analysis should take into account his basic narrative plan, his use of background material, complication, suspense, and climax and conclusion (when these two are divided). These parables may also be studied profitably with reference to some of the material that follows.

TECHNIQUES FOR GIVING NARRATIVE SPEECHES

Perhaps there is nothing more important to a good narrative than the use of dialogue (or direct discourse). Nothing helps the audience to enter into the original experience and relive it for themselves like dialogue. Dialogue enables the listener to hear it as it was. The parables of Jesus demonstrate a copious use of dialogue. In the parable of the Pharisee and the Publican, both prayers are quoted as spoken by each individual. In the story of the elder brother, found in Luke 15, verses 12, 21, 22ff. and 31, the use of direct discourse is illustrated. You may make a very fruitful study leading to an appreciation of the place of dialogue in the Scriptures by using a modern translation of the New Testament in which quotation marks are employed to designate direct discourse. Mark with a pencil every instance of the use of quotation marks in the Gospels. You will soon find that this is a laborious task. Such an exercise alone should deeply impress one with the importance of direct discourse in the Gospel narratives. Moreover, such a study would reveal that the parables of Jesus, which are narratives within those four greater narratives, are heavily freighted with the use of direct discourse. Instead of building more direct discourse into the exposition of those portions of the Scriptures in which there may be lesser amounts contained within the text itself (e.g., in some of the epistles), preachers not only fail to do this, but rather squeeze the life and vitality from those portions that are rich with direct discourse. Instead, they ring the passage dry and thus turn the living Word into a dull and uninteresting abstraction. This they proceed to toss out in this form to long-suffering and often diminishing congregations.

Someone at this point usually asks: "What do you do if there is only one person involved in the narrative? How can you get dialogue or direct discourse into the narrative then?" The answer is, you may use inner "dialogue," or soliloquy if you will. For example, in Luke 12:17 the rich man speaks to himself: "And he thought within himself, saying, 'What shall I do, since I have no place to store my crops?'" Verses 18 and 19 similarly continue the inner dialogue. In the parable of the elder brother, mentioned above, the younger (prodigal) brother speaks to himself:

"And when he came to himself, he said, 'How many hired servants of my father's have bread enough and to spare, and I perish with hunger!'" (Luke 15:17)

For other examples, note Luke 16:2ff. and 16:24.

Sometimes the use of dialect may be successfully employed as a refinement to the use of dialogue. But beware of the use of dialect wherever it might be offensive or would call attention to itself. As a general rule, whatever calls attention to itself detracts from the main point and, therefore, should be eliminated. Whenever there is any question about the propriety of the use of dialect, it is better to avoid it altogether. Remember Romans 14:23.

The value of specific details and concrete material in narrative speaking cannot be stressed strongly enough. Naming people and giving a description of individuals (at least incidentally) goes a long way toward making them three-dimensional and thus believable to the hearer. Characters in a narrative may be described, or labeled, or at least some characteristic may be noted. It is not wise to spend much time directly describing persons or objects unless the description is essential to an understanding of the main point. The rule of thumb to keep in mind is that wherever you may substitute a concrete detail for a generalization or an abstract term, by all means do so. The same object, for instance, may be called either a car (an abstract generalization into which each listener is forced to pour his own content) or a black '72 'Vette; a dog or a bulldog. Plainly the latter descriptions much more accurately describe what the speaker has in mind than the former. Make mental pictures definite. The more general term demands more participation by the listener, requiring him to fill in his own concept of what the word may mean. Frequently, therefore, he will paint the wrong picture, since he must paint out of his own most vivid past experience. He will use the colors he already has on his palette. The person who knows the facts, not the one who is trying to discover them, should mix the paint and wield the brush. Be concrete wherever possible. But it is important to remember that while all *helpful* details ought to be included, the "lace curtains" or details that are unnecessary to an understanding of the point of the story, should be eliminated. They will delay the unfolding of the story and detract and distract from the main point.

Humorous narratives are often very useful. If there is a choice between a narrative which says the same thing humorously and one that does not, choose the humorous story, unless, of course, the use of humor is inappropriate to the mood or the content of the talk and the occasion. It is almost always crucial when using humor to avoid the use of puns.

Preachers also must be careful not to poke fun at people. The simple and naturally humorous aspects of incongruity provide the best humorous material. Telling a joke on oneself at times may be appropriate.

USES OF THE NARRATIVE

There are many uses of the narrative. Narratives may be used to catch attention, to maintain interest, and to provide variety. When the listener has been taxed by sustained tension, a narrative may bring welcome relief by relaxing the tension. But these reasons in themselves are never adequate for introducing a narrative; they are the fringe benefits or by-products of the narrative. The reasons for which narrative is used are largely summed up under these three purposes:

1. To make a point vivid, clear or memorable.
2. To illustrate a principle or abstract truth in concrete, Monday morning terms.
3. To enable one to say through the narrative what a hostile audience might not accept otherwise.

To make the third abstract point clear and memorable we might illustrate by the story Nathan told David (II Samuel 12:1-4). First, Nathan gained David's assent to the principles involved in the story. Verses 5 and 6 indicate that the story had the desired effect. Then, through this story the Holy Spirit trapped David into conviction of his sin in order to bring him to confession. Had Nathan approached David directly about his sin, probably David would not have listened to him. But the story in which the point was made so clearly, and to which David had already implicitly given assent, enabled him to strike home at David's conscience with power: "You are the man!" (vs. 7). Similar use of parables by Christ is frequent in the New Testament (e.g., Matthew 21:33-46; note particularly vss. 40, 41, 45).

Everyone knows that narratives make a point vivid, vital and convincing. They help clarify and aid in retaining thoughts which, when stated abstractly only in the form of a principle might readily have been forgotten. Narratives may be used as introductions, as conclusions or as sub-points under major heads in sermons. Someone has said (while doing it himself) that in a sermon no major generalization should be made without a story or example by which it is illustrated.[2]

SOME FUNDAMENTAL INFORMATION
ABOUT DELIVERY

At this point it is important to begin to discuss delivery (the use of the voice and body) in a preliminary way, since good delivery is crucial in delivering a narrative speech. More must be said later on.

The basic narrative outline (previously discussed) also becomes the key to proper delivery.

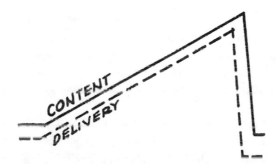

Figure 7
Delivery in Narrative Speaking
Delivery (use of voice and body) must
parallel content at each point.

You will notice in the diagram (Figure 7) that parallel to the particular elements of the basic narrative plan, at each point delivery follows content. This fact may be formulated

---

[2]In applying this rule, if you think you are introducing too many narratives into a sermon, you might check on whether you may not instead be introducing too many major generalizations.

as the most important rule about delivery: *content must determine delivery*. This order should never be reversed. Quite frequently, however, preachers do reverse the order with dire results. We have all seen the preacher who early in his career was told (wrongly) that he should smile and look pleasant while preaching. So, regardless of content, this pulpit Liberace speaks with a broad smile or leering grin (as it may variously be interpreted). Such a preacher will stand up with the broadest smile on his face and say, "Now let me tell you about my grandmother's funeral. . ." We have all also heard the preacher who believes that sermons should be shouted from the first syllable to the last. Such a preacher will arise and declare with a horrible cry, "God loves you!" Usually he will augment this verbal attack by shaking his fist in your face as he screams these words. It is unfortunate that preachers have fallen into such strange practices. In our day-by-day activities, normally we allow content to determine delivery. Who would think of proposing to his fiance by shaking his fist in her face and saying, "I love you" to the accompaniment of a shout or growl? As a preacher cannot speak effectively about hell while smiling, neither can he speak of the joys of heaven with a drab, dull, lifeless, stoical, unemotional attitude.

At each point, then, both the way that the voice is handled and the way that the body functions, must grow out of and parallel the content so that the delivery assists rather than hinders the transmission of the content. As a demonstration of how much content is conveyed through the use of the body alone (one of the two sides of delivery), simply turn down the sound on your TV set and watch the faces and bodily actions of the speakers.

The importance of delivery and its power to function as a negating factor is well known. By the mere wink of an eye, everything that one says may be reversed. By the unwitting "wink" of the body or voice, preachers frequently do the same. While they are talking about commitment or conviction or enthusiasm, by their own lackluster delivery they deny the very words that they speak. Such preachers unintentionally distort and deny the truths of the Scriptures as they attempt to preach them; their congregations hear not only what they say, but they also hear the way in which they say it. Often congregations just as unconsciously follow the subtle unintended message delivered by the preacher, that may be quite contrary to the Word of God. Sometimes theological students think that giving attention to pulpit speech is unimportant or "unspiritual." However, the facts about delivery demonstrate the vital importance of this study. Attention must be given to pulpit speech not in order to turn a preacher into a Demosthenes of the pulpit, but rather to keep him from distorting the Word of God. The effort in this book is to help the preacher to preach the Bible truthfully and effectively. Study of the use of speech in the Scriptures shows careful attention to this matter.

How, you may ask, can I learn to parallel content and delivery? In a narrative, for instance, how can I learn to vary delivery according to content by the unemotional presentation of background material, the more emotional introduction of complicating problems, and the emotional building of suspense? Is this done in some mechanical fashion, or is there another way? Can I think about such matters as I am preaching? Should I? These important questions must be answered. Not all of the answers need to be given at this point, but some basic guidelines may be established.

Good delivery arises naturally from one's attitudinal viewpoint. Body and mind function jointly; thought triggers emotion. In telling a story, preachers must learn how to *relive* rather than *report*. If the preacher takes his stand in today and looks back on the story as though it happened yesterday, he *reports*. The reporter, removed in time and space from the experience, tends to relate it dispassionately. However, if he returns in viewpoint to yesterday and brings his audience with him back into the experience as he tells it, both he and they will *relive* it; that is, the story will come alive for them. The speaker in telling the story should feel the chill or thrill of the experience running down his spine. He may be sure that when he himself can feel something of the fear or the joy or the anxiety or the perplexity of the moment *in his body,* then his congregation also is in a position to live through the experience. In other words, the preacher's delivery will parallel content when he gets his own emotions involved in the narrative content. In telling a narrative, the preacher must re-experience the narrative emotionally (never so fully that he loses control of his emotions, however). Within control, one must let himself go; i.e., let the content control his emotions. He must preach the scriptural content that is before him (some of which contains the most emotionally moving narratives ever penned) with the same emotion that the writer and the people experiencing the events felt as they lived through them. Vitality, animation, and enthusiasm characterize the effective delivery of a narrative, but these principles of delivery extend beyond the presentation of narratives to all pulpit speech. More must be said about delivery later on.

One final observation on delivery seems necessary. Apart from a serious organic problem, there is no excuse for a speaker not to be heard. We have all *learned,* as a habit, to speak at various intensities. Those who have difficulty in being heard have learned not to be heard. When a preacher cannot adequately fill a reasonably sized auditorium with the sound of his voice, it is because he has learned poor habits of speech. Fortunately, what was learned can be unlearned and new habits may be acquired. Every healthy child is born with the basic equipment to be heard. He demonstrates this early in his life when he is able to make himself heard through a brick wall by screaming at the top of his voice so that his mother can hear him when she is outside hanging up clothes. Often strapping men, now many times the size they were when they were born, even though their lungs have greater capacity and their vocal folds have expanded and lengthened, protest that they cannot speak more loudly than they do; yet they cannot be heard as far as the fifth pew. The protest is unfounded; the claim simply is untrue. Volume is a matter of learned behavior which can be changed.

IMPROVING DELIVERY

The basic question for such preachers to ask is, "How can I improve my delivery?" In answer, several helpful suggestions may be offered. We know a good bit about the process of learning and unlearning behavior. First, breaking old patterns and establishing new ones takes regular, patient practice. Second, practice should not take place during formal speaking situations, but rather in ordinary day-by-day speaking situations. Third, practice should take place in short sessions, five to fifteen minutes in length. Fourth, these short practice sessions must be held daily. Often it is wise to attach the sessions to some particular activity (like after eating a meal) that occurs regularly each day. Last, practice, of course, must involve correct practices. All that practice does is to fix habits, without asking if they are good. So if the practice involves engaging in faulty practices, the practice will be harmful rather than helpful.

Here is a concrete suggestion for profitable practice; promise to tell a story to your children each night. Now, you don't need to tell your wife or your children why you have decided suddenly to engage in this particular activity, but you may be sure that they all will love you for it (your congregation will be happy about the results as well). This scheme virtually assures regularity, since you may be sure that if you make the promise, your children and your wife will hold you to it. The suggestion has an additional advantage: when telling a story to children, you can try out anything, no matter how far out, and get away with it. Not only can you practice style (that is, language usage; you may reach out for new, simple, vivid words that children understand and that ordinarily are not a part of your speaking vocabulary), but your delivery particularly can be stretched. When telling stories to children, you may easily practice using your hands descriptively, emphatically and indicatively. You will be able to exaggerate your gestures and facial expressions to their limit without fear. You can try out all sorts of grunts and growls and groans and shouts, whistles and wheezes, and whatever else you like, all with great abandon and without the least suspicion about your sanity. You may experiment with the whole range of your vocal and physical potential, and the louder and wilder and the more experimental you become, doubtless, the more your children will enjoy it. It is hard to imagine a setting that offers as many built-in advantages for practice. Here is one of your better opportunities. I recommend it heartily.

In all such practice, what you are seeking is not the acquisition of oratorical skills peculiar to preaching and different from those common to ordinary conversation. Nor should you try to incorporate various predetermined gestures appropriate to each emotion into your repertoire as the elocutionists tried and failed to do. Rather, you are concerned about learning to preach with the same bodily actions and with the same use of voice that you naturally use in normal conversation. If you concentrate your efforts in practice upon reliving, you will thereby begin to bring those habits of delivery that are already natural to informal conversation into the more formal speaking situation. Try to become warmly involved in the content; plug in your emotions as well as your mind. As you tell the story, feel what you are saying; learn to experience the very emotions that you and other persons in the situation felt when the events actually took place. You do not have to be concerned then about learning all of the complex information available concerning the quality, the volume, the pitch, or the rate at which your voice operates in order to improve.

The interesting thing about the physiology of the voice is that when you learn to feel the emotions that grow out of content, the voice and the appropriate bodily action will follow along without your giving conscious attention to them. For example, if the introduction of the complication into the narrative immediately creates a very tense situation which then rises quickly to a climax, when you are reliving the story you will begin to feel tension instantly spreading to all of the muscles that control the vocal folds also. That will mean that automatically and without the slightest conscious effort, the vocal folds will stretch. Stretching the folds automatically changes the quality of the voice. Stretched folds are harder than relaxed folds; thus the quality of speech naturally becomes less mellow and more strident. When the folds are stretched by the emotion-controlled muscles they act like the strings of a violin; the tighter the string (or fold) the higher the pitch. Bodily tension, as it mounts, also often tends (in ways not quite so easily explained) to accelerate the rate of speech and raise the volume. In other words, as you concentrate on reliving and feeling the emotions appropriate to content, you will be pleased to discover that all of these physiological aspects of speech naturally take care of themselves. There is no need for you to think consciously, "Now I must raise my pitch level. I must speak more loudly here. I must accelerate my speaking rate. I must change the quality to a more strident sort." None of this even needs to come consciously to mind.

As a matter of fact, such thoughts must not be allowed to come to mind during the delivery of the sermon itself. During the delivery of the sermon the preacher must think only of God, of his congregation, and of the content of the Word from God which he is attempting to bring to them. He cannot think about how he is speaking or about methodology at all. It is self-defeating for a preacher to think about the delivery he is using when preaching, just as it is wrong to think of the consequences of what he is saying at this time. Where proper practice takes place during brief periods regularly observed day by day, you will soon find that the new habits begin to bleed over into one's speech during the rest of the day and eventually into the formal speaking situation as well. After daily concentrated effort, some marked differences will usually be noticeable after about three weeks. In six weeks, some permanent changes ordinarily may be effected. But continued growth thereafter can be assured only by continued practice, although the practice may be spaced out and less concentrated. Speech improvement (which means practice) of some sort should be the life-long endeavor of every preacher.

SUGGESTED PROJECTS
For Classroom or Study

In the Classroom

1. Telling a narrative. Time: 3 minutes.
   a. Choose a limited topic, one simple incident, describing an event in which you participated.
   b. Allow the story to unfold as it happened. Use the basic narrative plan (do not use flashback, etc.).
   c. Be concrete; use necessary detail and dialogue.
   d. Practice telling the story, particularly working on delivery and the climax.
   e. Note: No written manuscripts, outlines or notes will be allowed during the delivery of this narrative or any of the other speeches in this course. All speaking will be strictly extemporaneous (though not impromptu).
2. Begin keeping notes on principles of speaking. Lay out a sheet in two columns as follows and fill in the principles you discover while listening to your classmates and others speak.

This speech was effective because . . .	This speech was ineffective because . . .
1.	1.
2.	2.
3.	3.
etc.	etc.

In the Study

1. Using the same format that is suggested in No. 2 (above) keep notes on sermons, speeches on television, etc.
2. Plan to use a narrative in each of your next five sermons. Try to observe carefully the principles of good narrative style.

Chapter Three

PREACHING TO INFORM
(The Preacher as a Teacher)

Speaking in order to inform is one of the most important types of speaking; and it is basic to all good preaching. In ordinary conversation we all must speak to inform every day. You come home to your family and tell them what took place during the day. Members of the family respond by filling you in on what happened to them. You must give directions, explain your viewpoint on the news, set forth the ways and means of raising gerbils, and on and on. Sometimes life may seem to consist of nothing else but explanations, explanations, explanations and more explanations. Preachers likewise must explain the facts of the Scriptures to their congregations. Persuasion is built upon the foundation of information. The two can be distinguished only in emphasis. Each message will primarily seek to inform or persuade; but while it is possible to inform without persuading directly (all truth *implies* belief and action, however), it is impossible to persuade properly except on the basis of adequate information. The bread and butter work of speaking is in one sense the task of informative or (as it is sometimes called) expository speaking.

TWO ELEMENTS

Informative preaching requires two things: 1. Information (facts plus the speaker's interpretation of them), and 2. understanding (the interpretation by the listener of the data presented). Of course, the Holy Spirit must be at work in all to make it efficacious.

1. *Information.* Information means content as understood by the preacher. Research skills are required. Part of such research is the ability to judge what information is new or of vital importance to a particular congregation. In other

42

words, what is informative to one congregation may be old hat to another. Judgment is needed, however, to distinguish between old material that needs to be repeated and old material that is truly old hat. Judgment must be developed to determine how much brand new information a given congregation can assimilate at one time. The speaker who tries to inform an audience about matters already well known to them insults his audience and wastes their time. The preacher who tries to give information that is too advanced for his congregation before giving them adequate background information may snow them, but does not inform.[1] Information, therefore, means something worth learning, that meets needs, and that it is possible for a congregation to learn.

2. *Understanding.* Understanding means the congregation's understanding of the information that the preacher gives them. First, the speaker must understand the information; he must know clearly what he wants his congregation to know. Only then is it possible for the congregation to understand the information clearly, for they will (at best) only understand it as the speaker has understood it. It is very important, then, for him to know before he can show; he must get the goods before he can deliver the goods. On the other hand, there are many preachers who have the goods but cannot deliver it. We have all heard preachers who knew their subject, and we knew they knew it, but they couldn't put it across. Exposition, or informative speaking, then has to do with getting something into your head, then into other heads, with the least possible loss or addition in the transmission process.

THREE AREAS OF KNOWLEDGE

There are three areas of knowledge to which one may turn in order to find information about which to speak. On the

---

[1]Cf. Hebrews 5:11-14. Note how the writer has analyzed his readers precisely in this manner.

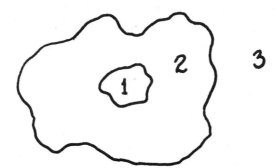

Figure 8: Three Areas of Knowledge: (1) Well-known, (2) Partially known, (3) Unknown.

diagram (Figure 8), area number 1 represents material that is so thoroughly known that one could be said to be virtually an authority on the subject. Area number 2 is very dangerous because we often think it comprises well-known information, whereas in reality this area embraces only partially known material. The preacher's knowledge of class 2 information is only more or less accurate, more or less detailed, more or less thorough; not known well enough to inform others about. So often speakers speak out of class 2 material as though they were speaking from class 1 material. Subtly, the distinction is blurred. And, of course, there is a third and larger area (3) that might be labeled "unknown." This is that vast area of information with which the preacher has only the slightest acquaintance. He has so little understanding of class 3 material that it would be impossible to speak about this information with the slightest semblance of authority or to convey anything meaningful about that material to another. The principle here is that nothing should be preached or taught before it has been brought within the scope, or at least very close to the edge, of area number 1.

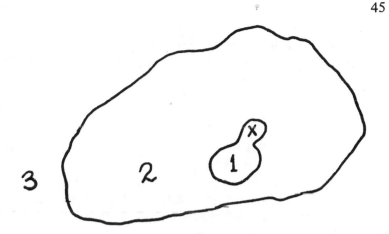

Figure 9
Broadening the Area of Well-known Material

You will notice that in the second information diagram (Figure 9), the border of the class 1 area has been expanded by research, study or whatever work was required, so that the preacher has brought within the pale of material known authoritatively, material (X) that previously belonged to class 2. In other words, to sum up, the preacher should speak only out of adequate preparation, study and research.

RESERVE POWER

The sort of research that brings information within the scope of area 1 also produces authority and power through what has been called "reserve power." Preparation that makes one something of an authority on a subject uncovers more material than can be used in any given sermon, and thus puts a person in possession of a reservoir of unused material. In some not altogether explainable fashion, that reservoir, like a reservoir of water, exerts a pressure that lends power to what he says. Congregations recognize reserve power (usually unconsciously) and, you may be sure, also know when it is lacking! Reserve power may be seen in various ways. A speaker with reserve power is able to answer questions about the details of his message. It is clear that he has not "shot his wad." He is not left with nothing more to say.

Informative speaking might tentatively be defined as speaking that orally transmits accurately understood information from the speaker to the listener in such a way that both understand the same information in the same way.

TRANSMISSION SKILL AND CLARITY

Everyone knows what clarity is, but all too few preachers know how to be clear. The roots of the words "say" and "see" are related. Saying should produce seeing. Our English phrase, "I see," used to acknowledge that one has understood, exactly makes the point. Clarity comes as the result of "informing" and "expounding" in their etymological senses. To inform, etymologically, is to "put something into its proper form." It is to make it take that form for the listener; it is to paint for him a picture of it like it is. Etymologically, to expound is to *set forth* or to *lay out* the facts, so that they can be seen. The picture in the word is similar to the one in our modern expression, "Lay the cards on the table." The image behind the word "expound" is about the same as that behind the words "make plain." To make plain, etymologically, is to *lay out on a flat, plain surface,* i.e., *where all can see plainly.* All of the images behind the words "expound," "make plain," and "inform," have in common the concept of making something clear by exposing it or showing it to be what it actually is.

OBSCURITY AND AMBIGUITY

Negatively speaking, clarity involves the removal of two factors: obscurity and ambiguity. Since it is essential in informative speaking to convey content with clarity, it is important to know how to avoid obscurity and ambiguity.

Obscurity is literally anything that covers up. There are many things which obscure or cover up content. First, *complexity* obscures. The informative speaker, therefore, must learn how to *simplify.* Long ago the cartoonists learned this art. Many of the cartoonists, with Walt Disney, found that if they omitted one of the four fingers and included only three fingers and a thumb they could get all of the action and expression they wished in the hands of cartoon characters. Drawing four fingers in cartooning at times can become quite complex. So they simply dropped one finger. Though people have read Walt Disney cartoons for years and years, most of them have never noticed this fact. The cartoonists lost nothing by dropping the finger; in fact simplifying, in this instance helped to clarify. In the process they replaced a thin little finger with a fatter, larger index finger that, for instance, can point directions more effectively. Similarly, simplification of concepts and ideas (in which there are resultant gains rather than communicative losses) must take place in preaching. Not *everything* about any subject can be said in every sermon. Therefore, eliminate what obscures. At times simplification allows for the enlargement of a major point that becomes the fat index finger of the sermon.

Secondly, *technical terms* may obscure. Technical terms obscure when they are unexplained or if they come too quickly or in too large a quantity. Doctors are perhaps the most obvious offenders in the use of unexplained technical language. Perhaps physicians can justify their use of Latin and Greek words on the grounds that they need a certain mystique and authority in order to get us to take their foul-tasting medicines and submit to the surgeon's knife. But preachers have no such excuses. You go to the doctor and say, "My head itches." After a few hmmm's he may say, "I'm afraid you have an acute case of pediculosis." Startled, you ask meekly, "Will I live?" He says, "Of course you will. All you'll have to do is get rid of those lice." Why couldn't he have said so in the first place? Why say pediculosis when you can say instead, "You've got lice"? Some preachers seem to think that technical terms, unexplained, will enhance their image. But the image of the preacher is unimportant compared to the clarity of his message. He must remember that his message is not his own; it is the message of God. The enhancing of a preacher's image at the expense of the Word of God is a capital offense. The Word of God is the simplest, most straightforward message in all the world. There are, of course, some technical terms in the Scriptures. These must be preserved, propagated, and explained. It is important for the members of our congregations to learn the great terms of the Christian faith, not only in order to read the Scriptures, but also to keep them in continuity with the best of Christian literature. Other technical terms ought to be used sparingly; and then never without explanation, and always in such a way that they can be learned and remembered.

Thirdly, *ornateness* obscures when it does not further the thought. Whatever does not further the thought calls attention to itself and thereby actually detracts from the message. Cleverness, the second cousin to ornateness, also obscures for the same reason. Preachers seem to be highly susceptible to the temptation to try to be clever in sermons. For example, many search Roget's *Thesarus* from cover to cover in order to find a third "r" or a fifth "l" or a fourth "p" simply for the sake of fancy alliteration. Finally, discovering that there is no third or fourth or fifth word that really fits, they settle for something that half fits, and as a result end up saying something different from what they really intended to say. What is more serious is that it is not what God said. So the message is distorted for the sake of cleverness. All such alliteration (most alliteration is boring and useless anyway) must be avoided.

The second factor that inhibits clarity is *ambiguity*. Ambiguity is anything that can be understood in more than one way. To be ambiguous because you said something poorly is bad, but to be ambiguous because you, yourself, are not sure about what you are saying is worse. We shall not speak of the ambiguity that results from the latter cause, since the solution to such ambiguity is repentance. However, ambiguity resulting from poor speech can and needs to be cleared up. The answers to ambiguity are: *precision* (which literally means to *cut off,* or to *sharpen*) and *accuracy* (which means to *take care*). Precision comes largely through concreteness, which involves the use of specific details and examples. Precision and accuracy also are aided by careful definition. It is of some importance to know what a definition, itself, is. Functionally speaking, a definition is that phrase or sentence which distinguishes one object or person from all others. Every good definition has four elements: (1) the term, (2) the verb *to be*, (3) a general classification, and (4) a particular classification. Thus, the four parts of a definition look something like this:

term	verb	general classification	particular classification
Delivery	is	those visible and auditory activities	by which the speaker communicates his ideas and feelings.

THE KNOWN AND THE UNKNOWN

Precision and accuracy may be enhanced by explaining the unknown in terms of the known. For instance, statistics are hard to understand unless they are visualized. Merely to state that the diameter of the moon is 2,160 miles really means very little to most people. How much more meaningful then to turn to the *World Book Encyclopedia* and find a drawing of the moon superimposed upon a map of the United States, with lines extended from its outer edges down to San Francisco and to Cleveland. The size of the known (the United States) adds tremendously to the understanding of the relative size of the unknown (the moon). Probably most readers were surprised to discover how small the moon actually is. Mere statistics do not show this, but placing the moon upon the map makes it quite clear. In another similar example, readers are pleased to discover in a book by Chester Warren Quimby entitled, *Paul for Everyone* (New York: Macmillan, 1947), that there is a map of Paul's journeys superimposed upon a map of the United States. Washington, D. C. becomes Antioch in Syria; Wilmington, North Carolina, becomes Jerusalem. One discovers that by land, Paul traveled as far north as Madison, Wisconsin (Philippi) and as far west as Marion, Iowa (Berea). By sea, he traveled west to Pierre, South Dakota (Rome) southwest to Hutchison, Kansas (Malta), and south centrally to Cairo, Illinois (Fair Havens). I would suspect that anyone who has just read these two descriptions of the moon and of the map of the Mediterranean will never forget them. Even though you have not seen the *World Book* illustration or a copy of Quimby's book, you will remember because of the explanation of the unknown in terms of the known. Often the mere juxtaposition of the known with the unknown makes a powerful impression. Preachers must learn to use this extremely important rule for clarifying new material. Scribes of the Kingdom of Heaven must bring out of their treasures things both old and new, said Jesus, and often they must bring the new truth in terms of the old story about known facts. With Christ learn to say, "The kingdom of heaven is like . . ."

THE ORGANIZATION OF INFORMATIVE SERMONS

Informative speaking must be adapted to the informative purpose, that is, to achieve the understanding and the retention of content through clarity. Persuasive speaking is aimed principally at belief or action; it is not primarily concerned with understanding (although understanding is essential to persuasion). The purpose determines the methodology. The purpose of persuasive speaking will require different methodology from that which is required by informative speaking. The big thing in informative structure is bold, rugged organization. When speaking informatively, let the bones protrude; make every rib show. Informative sermons should have rigid spinal columns. They are vertebrates, not jellyfish. While it is true that no sermon is exclusively informative or exclusively persuasive, we are talking now about its basic emphasis. The writer of the biblical passage upon which the sermon is based might particularly be concerned with getting information across. The preacher might, for example, be preaching from one of those portions into which Paul leads with the words, "I would not have you to be ignorant, brethren, concerning . . ." In such a passage, the Holy Spirit's purpose is plainly informative.

Some of the elements of bold, rugged organization are:

1. *Enumeration.* The use of numerical divisions like first, second, third (enumeration) especially aids in retention so long as there are not too many major points. Enumeration also clearly divides the various aspects of a subject.

2. *Repetition.* There is an old three-point rule of thumb which says, "Tell 'em what you're gonna' tell 'em; tell 'em; tell 'em what you told 'em." This basic deductive pattern is frequently useful. There are three stages in the development of a sermon using this plan: first you state the thesis (purpose or central idea), next you expand it, discussing it in detail, and then you summarize at the end. The plan is built on the principle of repetition. It is important to remember that a listener cannot reread a sermon as he can reread pages in a book. He must hear what you say the first time, at your speaking rate, according to your explanation. Any material of the sort that might require *rereading* in a book, in a speech must be *retold* by the speaker. In other words, you must help him to "reread" this material by *repeating* the material for him.

Information ought to be repeated in the same words and phrases only if these particular words and phrases are themselves of importance. Otherwise, most repetition is best given in different form. If the exact words are not important, then repetition in a different form allows you to approach the subject from another angle. When information is presented in various forms, a greater number of people with different experiences and backgrounds may more readily grasp it. Saying the same thing twice in different ways helps to clarify what is meant either the first or the second time. This is one of the values of the form of Hebrew poetry called synonymous parallelism. The second phrase (or term) of the parallel says roughly the same thing as the first but in different words. Frequently you can understand one or the other of the difficult terms in that parallel only by reading the other term.

What plans of organization are possible? There are various possible plans for bold informative speaking. Basically, all plans may be divided into those that classify and those that divide. Classification is the process of moving from diversity to unity, while division is the process of moving from unity to diversity. The sermon may sort out from a larger conglomerate those similar elements that fall into smaller groupings. Thus, the sermon may reveal the divisions (perhaps previously unrecognized by the congregation) of a subject. Or the sermon may group, out of a seemingly disorganized mass, those elements that are common to one another, classifying them under various heads.

One well-known plan for organizing the informative sermon is based upon the principle of comparison or contrast. Comparisons are similarities (classification). Contrasts are differences (division). Much of John's writing lends itself to this sort of organization, because John, himself, was fond of bold comparisons and contrasts.[2] Another method of organization in informative speaking uses time order: this plan utilizes such divisions as first, second, third, or ancient, medieval, modern. Space order provides a fourth way of organizing informative materials (also by division). For instance, the three accepted speech areas in the United States may be classified as the General American Speech Region, the Eastern American Speech Region, and the Southern American Speech Region. These basic informative plans may be used either alone or in combination. There are many other variations on these

---

[2]Cf. John's use of terms like: light/darkness, love/hatred, life/death, etc.

themes, but these should be found helpful in beginning to prepare an informative sermon.

TRANSITIONS IN INFORMATIVE SPEAKING

More will be said at another place about transitions. Transitions are important. Their purpose is to guide the listener smoothly from where he is to where you want him to go. A study of biblical transitions, especially in the epistles, reveals skill in the use of bridging diverse concepts; especially in linking doctrinal instruction to practical living and blending concrete ecclesiastical matters with doxology. A study of transition in the book of Revelation is particularly interesting.[3] One method of making transitions in informative speeches is by the use of the three-point transition, which consists of:

1. A summary of the past section
2. A transitional word or phrase
3. A brief introductory statement leading into the next section.

Here is an example of such a three-point transition: (1) Thus it is clear from all of these data that in the Old Testament era the mode of baptism was (without exception) sprinkling or pouring. (2) Now, (3) let's take a look at the New Testament evidence. . .

STYLE OF THE INFORMATIVE SERMON

Whitehead said, "A merely well-informed man is the most useless bore on God's earth." All of us know how desperately dull preachers can become at times when they try to teach. But the transmission of information certainly doesn't need to be dull. Rather, it can be exciting and interesting. Preachers must not become Bible butchers, chopping out great chunks of scriptural meat and throwing them raw and bloody to their

---

[3]Cf. Jay Adams, *The Time Is At Hand,* Philadelphia: Presbyterian and Reformed Publishing Company, 1969, pp. 20, 60, 68, 71, 83, 89.

congregations as if they were feeding tigers. There is nothing wrong with the meat. There is nothing wrong with the butchering process. But preachers must also learn to become cooks as well as butchers. They must learn to serve the meat well cooked, warm, well seasoned, garnished, with an appetizer and dessert, by candlelight. Most congregations choke and gag on a slab of raw doctrine, even if it is a prime cut. The preacher as butcher does research; the preacher as cook and host presents his materials in palatable, digestible, and inviting form.

INTRODUCTIONS

Let's take a look at that appetizer (introduction). Introductions should (as the word means) *lead into* the subject. Introductions should catch attention, arouse interest in and create a desire to learn more about the subject matter. In short, they should aid by evoking:

A - Attention

I - Interest

D - Desire

It is sometimes wise to assume that the audience is bored or is thinking about other matters, and that your first task is to arouse interest. Someone has said, "Light your match on the first strike." Often preachers waste a paragraph or two of words before getting into the subject. The trouble is that not only are words wasted, but members of the congregation are being turned off before they were ever really turned on. The first sentence should usually be gripping, if not striking. My wife has an appetizer that always draws comment. It is tomato juice spiked with ginger ale. Why not spike your introduction with something that has a bite? One man giving a speech on safety used as his first sentence these words: "Four hundred and fifty shiny new coffins were delivered to this city last Thursday." In a class on psychology the professor at the beginning of the period whipped out two pistols, fired blanks at the audience, and then declared, "Today I shall speak about stimuli and response."

It is possible for the introduction to be too graphic or too striking. If the introduction has so much of a bite that the rest of the sermon cannot measure up to it, then, instead of leading into the subject, it calls attention to itself and draws the listener away from the subject. A good introduction must be followed by a good sermon, or the rest becomes a letdown. But why shouldn't it be followed by a good sermon?

The key to an introduction, remember, is to move the congregation from wherever it is at the moment to where the preacher wants them to be. It is not sufficient, therefore, for the introduction simply to arouse attention or interest. As a good appetizer goes with the rest of the meal, so too an introduction must have a direct bearing upon the message that follows. It is easy to arouse interest. A preacher may appear before his congregation on Sunday morning carrying a strange box. Dramatically, he may open the box and let loose three pigeons. But while the bewildered congregation is watching these birds flap around in the auditorium, he, of course, could not preach. He, himself, would have destroyed any opportunity to speak. It is important, therefore, to prepare introductions carefully, usually after the rest of the sermon is well in hand, so that the direct relevance of the two is assured. In their introductions, preachers who fail to do so have opened boxes and let fly speckled birds of every sort.

A good introduction may, for example, answer the question, "Why bring that up?" After all, the speaker is asking the listener to consider a topic about which he has not been thinking. To change his thoughts is not always easy. Indeed, he may need help to do so. The introduction should provide this kind of help. Showing why it is important for him to turn his attention to this matter may be just what he needs. Few preachers, unfortunately, seem to bother about this problem and assume, often wrongly, that people are automatically interested in what they have to say. Senator Pat McNamara wisely showed the present importance of his subject when he opened an address with these words: "Of all the persons who have ever reached the age of 65 since the dawn of mankind, twenty-five per cent are alive today." One way to become conscious of the elements of good introductions is to study carefully the opening words in magazine articles.

Here are the introductory sentences to several sermons. What do you think of each?

1. "The first thought which seems to be suggested by these words (the words of his text) is a thought directly contradictory to a very prevalent opinion."

2. "You probably saw the advertisement, too."

3. "The words, 'a still small voice' are even more surprising in the original: 'a sound of thin silence.'"

4. "If you're a Christian, you can't say can't."

5. "James identified one cause of man's trouble, personal and social, when he said, Ye have not, because ye ask not.'"

6. "Do I have the money to give?"

7. "There was some danger in attending church when this exhortation (Hebrews 10:25) was penned."

CONCLUSIONS

While it is important to have a good appetizer, it is also essential to have a good dessert (conclusion). In informative speaking, the key to a good conclusion is repetition and summary, i.e., saying it again, "telling 'em what you told 'em." In the summary it is of special importance to repeat key words and phrases that should be remembered. The ending should contain the meat or gist of the message. A summary should tie up any loose ends, integrate thoughts, and focus upon the core of the message. It should be written in conjunction with the introduction and perhaps will wrap up the package in the same terms or imagery as was used in the introduction. End strongly; do not do a fade-out. Do not approach the landing field three or four times, only to soar up into the blue again at the last second. Instead, when the congregation has been alerted to fasten seat belts (by a "finally" or some similar signal) bring her in for a full flap landing on the first approach.

VISUAL AIDS

There are two kinds of visual aids: three-dimensional and two-dimensional. Many preachers, if they think of visual aids at all, limit their thinking to two-dimensional aids, such as chalkboards, charts, posters, graphs, pictures, slides, maps, overhead projectors, etc. But we should keep in mind the possibility of using three-dimensional aids as well. In fact, most of the visual aids used by biblical preachers were, according to the Scriptures, three-dimensional. Three-dimensional aids include both objects, like Agabus' belt (Acts 21:11), and people (cf. Matthew 18:2, 3). Objects may include either the actual items themselves or models scaled up or down.

There are two basic rules for the use of visual aids. The first is that *they must be visual.* This might seem to be a truism, yet those who have had anything to do with the study of visual aids know that frequently the visual aid is not large enough for everyone to see. Sometimes the visible qualities are obstructed by clutter. Detail tends to run together. The rule is to simplify in every way possible. For instance, it is frequently unnecessary to write out words; instead they may be abbreviated, the first letter of the word may be used, or symbols may be substituted for words. Second, when using a chalkboard, use bold, suggestive strokes. Heavy, confident and quick strokes with chalk or a magic marker are superior to time-consuming, thin, sketchy, carefully worked out lines. Third, you may want to exaggerate the size of some item in the drawing if you want to emphasize it. Of course, this should not be done if the exaggeration causes a distortion that misrepresents. Fourth, when you use colors in charts, on the board, etc., use bold primary colors that contrast, not pastels that tend to fade into one another. That is one reason why yellow chalk against a green blackboard is so effective. And, finally, when you use the aid, don't get in its way, don't stand in front of it, don't hold it so that it wiggles and shakes, but prop or tack or hang it up carefully so that it can be seen by all. Stand off to the side and point to the aid with your hand or with a pointer.

Figure 10
Simplify and Exaggerate

The second rule is that *visual aids must aid.* There is no middle ground here. They either aid or they hinder. They either help or they detract. Use only one aid at a time. Any aid which is not in use but is in view may detract. It is usually wise to cover and hide aids whenever possible, both before and after use. Second, the aid must be mastered. For instance, one must learn how to pull chalk rather than push it, so that it doesn't squeak and send shudders down the listeners' spines. The preacher must know his aid and, if possible should practice using it in the place where he will speak. I once saw a girl captured by a visual aid. Because it was a rainy day she had rolled up her poster and carried it across the campus to Switzler Hall, the oldest building at the University of Missouri. When she got up from her seat she marched confidently to the front of the room, produced two thumb tacks, and unrolled her poster. But as she pushed the first thumbtack into the poster board and attempted to tack the poster into the hardwood molding around the blackboard, she met strong resistance. The wood was so hard that she couldn't make the tack penetrate it. After several unsuccessful attempts, she valiantly put a hand at the top of the poster board in order to hold the aid against the blackboard herself. But the poster was rolled tight, and when she unrolled it, the poster acted exactly like one of those stiff white shirts that is worn with a tuxedo. Every time she tried to smooth it out and unroll the board, it rerolled itself, recoiling up toward her hand at the top of the poster. Finally, when all else failed, in desperation she grasped the bottom of the poster with her free hand, and with that move had been completely captured by her aid. One final word of warning: never talk to the aid—always speak to people.

CONCLUSION

Now, as we said, comes the time for a summary. A good summary contains key words and phrases. The big word in informative preaching is *clarity. Information* is the material with which the preacher works, *understanding* (and *retention*) is the goal that he seeks, and *clarity* is the means by which he attains this goal. Now abideth these three: information, understanding and clarity; but the greatest of these is clarity. As the professor said: "If I can get this one word into your head, you'll have it all in a nut shell."

SUGGESTED PROJECTS
For Classroom or Study

In the Classroom

1. Using one of the topics chosen earlier (or some other), prepare a 5-minute talk on a subject about which you believe your audience needs to be informed and about which you have (or plan to acquire) adequate knowledge.

2. Hand in a one-page full sentence outline at least two days before you must speak (you may continue to revise this until the moment of delivery), containing the following elements and using this form:

TITLE

PURPOSE: (Here follows a one-sentence statement of the specific purpose of this talk: e.g., "I wish to tell my audience how we got the present chapters and versification in our Bibles.")

INTRODUCTION: _____. _____.

_____.

   I. _____.

     A. _____.

       1. _____.

       2. _____.

     B. _____.

       etc.

  II. _____.

    etc.

CONCLUSION: _____. _____

_____. _____.

Remember: During this course no notes or outlines may be used while speaking. You may use visual aids during this speech or any that follow, if you elect to do so.

In the Study

Using the outline form suggested in No. 2 (above), prepare an informative talk that could be given to your Sunday school teachers on The Use of Visual Aids.

Chapter Four

PERSUASIVE PREACHING
I–PREACHING TO CONVINCE

Fundamentally, there are two types of persuasive sermons. The first type involves what might be called argumentative preaching, and the second motivational preaching. The goal of argumentative preaching is to convince. This means changing and establishing a belief. Of course, ultimately only the Holy Spirit can convince. Yet the very fact that he has given to his Church the office of pastor and teacher (Eph. 4:11) shows that he plans to use preaching as the agency through which he accomplishes his work.[1] The human means that the Holy Spirit ordinarily uses is the use of logical scriptural proof of the sort employed by Paul and Peter throughout the Book of Acts and in their letters. This means interpreting biblical evidence and reasoning from it to sound, practical conclusions. The goal of motivational preaching, on the other hand, is to move to action. Whereas the preacher primarily aims at the intellect in argumentative persuasion, in motivational persuasion he aims through the intellect at the emotions. The same means are used in both, with the important exception that when he seeks to move to action, the preacher must also employ psychological appeal.

BIBLICAL PERSUASION

Some persons try to be more pious than Paul; but their piety is false. They say that persuasion in preaching is unnecessary and the implication, therefore, is that those who use persuasion ignore the Holy Spirit and depend upon the arm of flesh. "Simply present the facts," they maintain, "and let the Holy Spirit do the rest." However, that viewpoint is de-

---

[1]Cf. Adams, *Competent to Counsel,* Chapter II, pp. 20-25.

cidedly unscriptural. It was Paul's regular custom *(eithos)* to "argue" *(dielexato)* from the Scriptures (Acts 17:2). The word *dielaxato* comes from *dialego,* which means to reason, discuss, or dispute. In Acts 17:3, Luke notes two of the elements that are involved in this dialectical method that Paul developed: he "explained" *(dianoigon,* or "fully opened") and "proved" *(paratithemenos,* "demonstrate" or "set before"). The effect of these joint activities is also described in verse 4, where Luke observes that some were "persuaded" *(epeisthesan).* These words plainly describe a process of reasoning through argumentation; Paul is involved in changing people's thinking by this process. Paul set forth the scriptural evidence and argued from it. By this process the preacher endeavors to move someone from doubt to acceptance by means of biblical data presented logically in verbal form. Of course, it is important to recognize that the whole process used in reasoning with facts (evidence) rests upon the bedrock of assumptions or presuppositions that are agreed upon explicitly or implicitly by the speaker and his listeners. It is important also to notice that persuasion was not some extraordinary activity in which Paul infrequently engaged; this method of preaching had become customary (verse 2). Indeed, in Acts 17:17 Luke says that he argued *(dielegeto)* in the synagogues and in the market places every day. In Acts 18:14 he is pictured as arguing in the synagogue each Sabbath. Plainly, then, argumentation was a regular part of Paul's missionary preaching. It was a definite part of the gospel presentation. Throughout the book of Acts, from the second chapter on, wherever gospel preaching by Peter, Stephen, or Paul is recorded (at least as a summary), it is plain that the Scriptures of the Old Testament are used as the basis for such reasoning. New Testament preachers reached their positions concerning Jesus Christ by showing how he had fulfilled the Old Testament prophecies in history. In summarizing his missionary work, Paul put it this way: "Knowing the terror of the Lord, we persuade *(peitho)* men" (II Cor. 5:11).

There is a different word in the New Testament that signifies the wrong sort of persuasion. This word is used in Acts 18:13 and means "persuasion by deceit" or "misleading persuasion" (the word used here is *anapeitho*). In I Corinthians 2 Paul does not argue against reasoning or argumentation in general. He says that he had determined to "know nothing but Christ and him crucified" among the Corinthians. In order to assure this, he made certain that his message and preaching were not in *peithois sophias logois* (vs. 4); that is, he refused to use "persuasive words of wisdom" (here he means the wisdom of men as he has defined this in the previous chapter[2]). He wanted their faith to depend instead upon the demonstration and power of the Spirit. But from what Luke tells us, we know that this cannot mean that he refused to persuade by arguing from the Scriptures. Notice also Paul's stress upon the wisdom of men in verse 5.

The Spirit has given his Word to men not to be ignored, but to preach and be believed. The Spirit is the One who makes known the truth of God and the Gospel (compare vss. 12, 13, 14, 15, 16); thus it is impossible for one man to convert another simply by means of persuasion. But this does not preclude the fact that the Spirit may work, if and when he wills, through persuasion. Indeed, he ordinarily chooses to demonstrate his truth through the "foolishness" of the kind of persuasive preaching that is based upon reasoning from the Scriptures where the wisdom of God may be found. This is what Luke says Paul did; it is also what Paul did in Corinth. It is not persuasion, then, that Paul opposed (cf. Acts 28:23 and 19:8); his words in I Corinthians 1 are directed against the sophistical methods that many other teachers of his day employed. These methods focused upon eloquence and reasoning itself rather than upon the truth about Christ and his

---

[2]Indeed, the Kurt Aland text brackets *logois* and reads simply, *en peithoi sophias* ("with persuasive arguments of wisdom"). The stress is not against persuasion, but rather against persuasion by worldly wisdom.

atoning death. It is all such trickery and specious argumentation as that used by the sophists that Paul rejects. His very concern arises from the fact that in preaching the Gospel he *did* have to argue. He trembled because he was afraid that he might be tempted to argue in such a way that their faith might rest upon human wisdom. The kind of persuasion that Paul believed in and practiced, pointed men to the Christ of the Scriptures. In the rest of this chapter he makes it very plain that even *such* reasoning, apart from the regenerating work of the Spirit in the heart, is hopeless. So that even scriptural reasoning cannot bring about conversion apart from the Holy Spirit. No man can savingly say "Jesus is Lord" except by the Spirit (I Cor. 12:3). But biblical argumentation is one of the means of grace that the Spirit of God uses in bringing the elect to repentance and faith.

THE PROBLEM IN PERSUASION

The problem in logical persuasion (argumentation) is how to move the listener from doubt to acceptance, or at least how to move him further along the way toward acceptance. Frequently, the beginner harbors the mistaken notion that he ought to be able to convince most of his congregation to see things his way (which hopefully is also God's way) by means of a single sermon. This, of course, may happen, but usually it does not. Ordinarily, Christians move from doubt to acceptance over a period of time. And that is not altogether bad. Believers should "test all things (including sermons) and hold fast to what is good" (I Thess. 5:21).[3] When the Scriptures are consistently and clearly presented bit by bit, piece by piece, Christians will grow; they will come to understand and believe more and more, sometimes in spite of themselves. So,

---

[3]Cf. Acts 17:11. The Bereans had already learned this lesson. If a congregation is cautious and checks you out scripturally, with Paul, you should rejoice and praise them for it. Beware of those who too readily accept everything you preach.

a realistic goal ought to be set for each sermon. Set goals in terms of what one particular sermon of a given sort ought reasonably to be expected to accomplish. Then, if the Spirit "does exceedingly abundantly above what you ask or think," rejoice. Then he, and not you, will have the glory for the results.

The words that are used to describe various aspects of logical persuasion are themselves informative. The etymology of the English word *argue* may be found in a root meaning "to make clear." The fact that making something clear is a way of arguing shows the importance of clarity, not only when attempting to inform, but also in the process of argumentation. As a matter of fact, many people accept a statement as true if they understand it. So, clarity is essential in argumentation. Or to put it another way, argumentation must be built upon the foundation of the principles of informative speaking that we have studied already. It is not by departing from the use of facts and evidence in argumentation, but by building on them that you may progress to persuasion. The word *evidence* comes from two terms that mean "to see" and "out." These two words compounded mean that evidence is that which helps one to see out there in front of himself where he can see it plainly or clearly. The word *proof* comes from a root that means "that which can stand the test." And finally, *reason* originally meant "to think" by joining or fitting pieces together. The process of joining is analogically used to describe the thinking process as joining bits of evidence together with the cement of reasons in order to reach conclusions. So the words themselves that are employed in the process of persuasion say a great deal about the process itself.

CHOOSING AN ARGUMENTATIVE SUBJECT

In a preliminary course in pulpit speech you are not yet ready to preach. Probably you will be wondering how to choose a subject for this course. In choosing such a subject the first consideration might be the audience. When Dr. Martin Lloyd-Jones determined to preach his famous series on the Sermon on the Mount, he did so not because of his own interests ("If I had been left to my own choice I would not have chosen to preach [this] . . . series of sermons"). Rather, the needs of the church demanded it.[4] It will often be necessary to do an audience analysis to discover needs, problems, beliefs, attitudes, prejudices and errors. The choice of the subject should be made in the light of such information. Choose a topic that puts you in a position to grapple with the beliefs of your audience. Be sure you believe what you are saying to be true, but also be sure that most of your audience does not.

Secondly, the subject must be limited sufficiently to enable you to do a satisfactory job. The topic should be narrow enough (perhaps some mildly controversial *aspect* of a subject about which you all agree) to reasonably expect some noticeable (though possibly small) shift in belief if the speech is successful. Unless the subject is fairly well narrowed, a speech cannot possibly cover the following four factors, all of which are essential to good persuasion:

1. *Explanation of the state of the argument.* You often need to consider most or all of the following items: What is the problem specifically? Why is this problem important? What are the positions that have been taken and now are taken with respect to this question? By whom? What is the history of the argument? What are the definitions of key terms used in this argument?

2. *Evaluation of your own arguments.* Are they sound? Is the evidence factual? Are your sources reliable? Are your interpretations correct? Is your reasoning unassailable? Do you understand your own position clearly? Are there weak points or fuzzy thinking? Are you fully convinced yourself? Ques-

---

[4]D. M. Lloyd-Jones, *Studies In the Sermon on the Mount, Vol. I,* William B. Eerdmans Publishing Company, Grand Rapids, 1960, p. 9.

tions like these will not only help you to anticipate objections and enable you to shore up your defenses, but, because they demand a reevaluation of your position, sometimes will cause you to refine and modify it, and sometimes to reject it. Many of the results of such an evaluation of your position will become part of the positive presentation and argumentation for it.

3. *Refutation of your opponent's arguments.* Both his constructive arguments and his attacks upon your position must be anticipated. You must know what he will say for his viewpoint and also what he will say against yours. You will thereby provide ammunition to use in anticipation and also much with which to answer his objections at a later point. By anticipating and pre-answering in your initial presentation, you preempt him and remove much of the force of what he might say. A strong argument, then, is not merely an argument for, but must also be an argument against. Note especially how Paul anticipates objections and counter-arguments when he writes, "You will say to me then . . ." (Rom. 9:19; see also 11:19, I Cor. 15:35 and James 2:18).

4. *Summary and appeal.* Taking time to summarize so that the impact of the full argument is felt is important. Moreover, it is essential to urge acceptance upon the audience. This point becomes particularly crucial when persuading to move to action, so further discussion of it will be reserved until you reach that point.

When you have a subject that satisfies these criteria and about which you are confident that you can speak effectively because there is time to cover most or all of them, then your subject is properly limited. When a subject is too broad, you will discover that there is not enough time for all of these things within the framework of the talk. Not all speeches will require blanket coverage of all of these items. Some items may be conceded by the opposition since some facts may be mutually accepted by all parties.

FOUR TYPES OF DISPUTABLE QUESTIONS

Thirdly, it may be helpful to recognize that there are four categories of disputable questions from which a topic may be chosen. There are questions of (1) *fact*—does it exist? The woman's question, "Is not this the Christ?" (John 4:29) fits this category; (2) *definition*—what is its nature? Pilate's "What is truth?" (John 18:38) probably belongs to this class; (3) *value*—what is it worth? (cf. I Cor. 15:29a, 32). These three types of questions are all appropriate for the argumentative speech to convince; (4) *policy*—what action should be taken? (cf. Acts 2:37). A persuasive speech of this sort is motivational and is not presently of interest to us. Statements or questions of policy can be recognized by the fact that they usually contain the word "should" or the word "ought."

TYPES OF ARGUMENT

There are two basic kinds of arguments: the *inductive* and the *deductive* argument. When arguing inductively one moves from particulars to generalizations. Inductively organized sermons are like the locusts of Revelation; they have the sting in their tail. For instance, if you wish to preach about limited atonement to an audience that is hostile to the doctrine, you might be wise to argue inductively. You may begin by saying, "Christ is a personal Savior: 'He loved *me* and gave himself for *me*,'" quoting Galatians 2:20b. You may then argue that God's purposes are never frustrated, and quote various passages to support this fact. You may also suggest that it is unthinkable (because unbiblical) that at the very same moment that Christ was dying for their sins multitudes were themselves suffering in hell for the same sins. You may further establish biblically that Christ came to save, not merely to make salvation possible, and that his death indeed does pay the penalty for the sins of those for whom he died. You may wish to explain that his atonement was not merely the storing of potentially redemptive energy that may or may not be tapped, but that it was an actual payment of a debt. You may show in Isaiah 53 and in the New Testament Christ is said to "die" or "give his life" or "shed his blood" for *many*. At the very end you would draw all of these points together to their inevitable conclusion (generalization) that the atonement must have been limited and not universal.

A deductive argument moves in the opposite direction. It moves from a generalization to particulars. For instance, you may set forth your thesis immediately in the introduction to your sermon: "Today I intend to show that the biblical mode of baptism is by sprinkling and never by immersion. Your first point might be: Baptism in the Old Testament was always by sprinkling. Under that head you might turn to Hebrews 9:10 and compare Numbers 8:7, showing that the "different kinds of *baptismois*" in the Old Testament to which Hebrews 9:10 refers, are identified in the rest of that chapter as "purifications." You would then show that Old Testament purifications, according to Numbers 8:7, were accomplished by the sprinkling of the water of purification. You may also show as your second point under the first main head that John 3:25, 26 identifies baptism with Old Testament purification. This leads again to the conclusion that it is the sprinkling of the water of purification to which the Bible refers whenever it speaks of prechristian baptisms. Thirdly, you may also wish to point out that there is no act even resembling an immersion required by the Old Testament Law, let alone "various types" of immersions; yet Hebrews 9:10 says "different kinds of baptisms" were required. So there could not be various types of immersions. But throughout the ninth chapter of Hebrews, there are clear references to various purifications by sprinkling. There is the sprinkling of water and blood (vs. 19), the sprinkling of blood alone (vs. 21) and the sprinkling of blood and ashes (vs. 13).

As your second main head you could maintain: "Baptism in the New Testament was always by sprinkling." You might show that John the Baptist sprinkled, observing that the John 3 passage, where his activity is denominated as "purification," makes this clear. You might show that the passage also does not teach that there was "much water" in Aenon (as the King James Version wrongly translates verse 23) but literally "many waters" *(hudata polla).* These "waters" can be identified more specifically: the passage says that John was baptizing "in Aenon because there were many waters there." The word Aenon means "springs." All you need to do then is to put two and two together, and so on and on. The whole argument may continue throughout a number of the other key New Testament passages in which you may show that there is never a single allusion to baptism by immersion, but always baptism by sprinkling. You move successively through Acts 2, 10, Romans 6, Colossians 2, etc., showing that the biblical mode is described as "sprinkling, coming down upon, resting upon, shedding forth, pouring out and an anointing." Finally you conclude: "As I said when I began, the testimony of the whole Bible is clear: baptism was always by sprinkling."

Now, if you were going to deliver this message before the Orthodox Presbyterian General Assembly, a deductive method of this sort would be highly advisable. It would give you the advantage of repeating the thesis again and again throughout the whole message, reinforcing what the members of the Assembly already believe. It might possibly add new arrows to their quiver. There would be no opposition to overcome.

But suppose you were invited to speak before the Southern Baptist Convention and had elected to preach on the same subject! Here you would be wise to approach the question inductively, or probably you would not get beyond the introduction. Turn this outline on the mode of baptism inside out, and you have an inductive presentation. Instead of beginning with the thesis that baptism was by sprinkling both in the Old Testament and in the New, using the same approach as in the outline of the sermon on Limited Atonement (note also the inductive title: Christ, Our Personal Savior), you might begin by saying, "Let's look at some passages on baptism." You take a look at Hebrews 9 and ask some questions; you look at

John 3 and come up with some puzzling information. Then you look at baptism in the New Testament and you discover more interesting facts. All along you have been drawing some minor conclusions; now you must finally conclude that "as amazing as it may seem, the biblical evidence indicates that in both the Old and New Testaments baptism was by sprinkling alone."

The advantage of the inductive method is that you will get a hearing. Stephen was stoned, but not before he got his message across. Paul, likewise, got a hearing in Athens. In both cases an inductive approach assured this.[5] In general, then, audience analysis is all important in determining the type of argumentative approach to use. Ask yourself, "What kind of attitude does the audience have toward me and my proposition?" when you can answer that, you will know whether your approach ought to be inductive or deductive. Must you approach them as Nathan confronted David, or can you move directly to your thesis? Hostility indicates induction, friendliness indicates deduction.

TYPES AND TESTS OF EVIDENCE

The basic information used in preaching comes from the biblical revelation. Since the Bible is an inspired and inerrant document in the original, the only test that may be applied to this information is the test of the preacher's interpretation and use of it. There are two problems that arise in handling scriptural data: first, the preacher must determine what the Scriptures teach. While the Bible does not err, the preacher's interpretation may. Secondly, the preacher must determine the Holy Spirit's purpose in revealing the particular data under consideration and determine what legitimate use he may make of these facts today. There is also non-revealed factual

---

[5]Cf. Christ's use of this method in Matthew 21:28-32. Like Nathan, through the use of a parable, he gains consent for the principle that he is about to apply to his audience.

material of several sorts. Such material may not only be mis-interpreted and misused, it may also be false. More needs to be said about using and testing the several sorts of non-re-vealed material. First consider the problems connected with one highly specialized kind of material:

Statistics. Statistical materials can be quite tricky. First, it is essential to be precise in the use of statistical material. It is usually not adequate to say a "few" or "many" or "some." It is far better to say five, eighty-four or three-fourths. Listeners understand statistical materials most easily, we have seen, when they are translated into concrete terms. It is often wise to use comparisons: "as large (small) as . . ." or direct trans-lations: "If all of these were placed side by side, they would stretch from New York to . . ." Statistical materials need to be tested. This may be done in a variety of ways. For exam-ple, since it is wise for a listener to evaluate the sources of statistics, preachers need to learn to cite sources. In source evaluation one should want to know such facts as whether the sources are expert or lay, biased or disinterested, and if they were in a position to know. He will also question the quantity and quality of the information behind the statistics. Was there a broad enough sampling? Did it really cut across all of the classes or areas involved? So statistics themselves are very slippery and, unless quite simply presented togeth-er with some evaluation about quality, source, and meaning, often the listener is unable to judge their actual value.

Example. Examples are used in argumentation as support-ing pieces of evidence for the general proposition that is drawn from them. It is especially important for preachers to learn to use examples because while they support, at the same time they clarify, illustrate and frequently by their concrete-ness apply. The effective use of example by Christ as his most pointed means of argumentation should encourage every min-ister to seek to excel in their use. In effect, the Gallup Polls use numerous examples in arriving at statistics. Examples become support when they are clearly typical of numerous occurrences and truly illustrate and support the thesis.

One question to ask might be, "Is the example full?" That is, is the example a narrative or merely the reference to a narrative? The latter is called an "instance." Sometimes it is more effective to pile up instances than to present one or two full examples (cf. Paul in II Cor. 6:4-10). Another essential question is, "Is the example real or is it hypothetical?" Hypothetical examples may not be used for support in the way real examples may. Therefore, we want to ask, "For what purpose is it used? To support a thesis? To clarify the point? To help listeners retain information? To catch and hold attention?"

We should test the use of examples by questions like these: Are there enough cases cited? Are these cases typical? Is there a fair cross section? Are exceptions noted? Can predictions be made for the next specific case? And, the crucial rule of all, do the examples relate to the point at issue?

Analogy. Analogy proceeds on the assumption that since two things are alike in some *essential* respects, they will be alike in *other* respects. The issue here is, are they really alike in the essential respects? You have a comparison between cases. If a particular church extension program worked well for the Conservative Baptists, can it be argued that it would also work for the Orthodox Presbyterians? Analogies may be literal or figurative, and may be used respectively as proofs or illustrations. Voting a church officer out of office may be used as a literal analogy, but changing horses in mid-stream is a figurative analogy. Can you, for example, parallel something that takes place in education with something that takes place in medicare or in a church Sunday school? If so, you would be using a literal analogy. Can you argue that because of moral decay America is on the verge of collapse as a world power because imperial Rome fell due to inner corruption?

Cause. Then there is the argument from cause. The argument from cause expresses a reason for the being of a fact. It moves from cause to effect in predicting the future or from effect to cause in discussing the why of the past. Cause to effect runs this way: if we do *this*, then *that* will follow. Effect to cause says: Rome fell *because* so and so took place. Here the argument may be tested by asking questions like these: Is the cause-effect connection broken or incomplete? Will another cause change the predicted event? Are there additional causes contributing to the effect? What other effects might be produced by the cause? A speech teacher shatters a piece of chalk against the chalkboard and asks, "What is the cause of the resultant spot on the chalkboard?" From one viewpoint the chalk may be said to be the cause; but also the physical nature of the board is the cause; the course in speech is the cause, the class is the cause, and the instructor is the cause. Each is a cause at a different level. When discussing cause and effect, you must understand what you mean by the words.

Sign. Relations and associations that cannot be stated causally nevertheless are used as the reason for believing in the being of a fact. For example, when you see robins you say that spring has arrived. The Scriptures speak of the budding of the fig tree as a sign (Matt. 24:32-34). Where there is smoke there is fire; where there are pickets, there is a strike, are other examples of sign. The miracles of Jesus Christ are literally called "signs."[6] They were performed to attest to his Messiahship (Acts 2:22). Christ argued from sign to reassure John the Baptist when he doubted in prison. Compare Matthew 11:2-6.

The tests of a sign are: Are qualifiers used, such as "some, few, many, most"? Qualifiers may indicate only exceptions rather than rules. Do the signs show probability or only accidental association? For instance, a red nose may be the sign of drinking, sunburn, a cold, a punch in the nose, etc. There

---

[6]Cf. John 20:30-31 and throughout the book. In Mark 2:10 the miracle which involved the "*power* of the Lord" (*dunamis;* cf. Luke 5:17b) was a sign of his "authority" *(exousia).* Christ argues that the miracle is a visible, tangible sign of his invisible, intangible authority to forgive sins.

may be multiple causes for a particular sign. Are signs mistaken for causes? A sign is a sign of the existence of a problem, but not necessarily a sign of the specific item that is the cause of the problem. Depression may be the sign of guilt, but it does not indicate the specific nature of the guilt. To put these various types of argument together in one sequence, you may proceed to argue in this order: *signs* indicate that a proposition is true; the *causal arguments* indicate why it is true; and the *examples* support and convince, while the *analogy* helps us to understand in terms of what is already known by the listener.

THE STOCK ISSUES, A STRUCTURAL TEST

Stock issues, as they have been called by debaters, are helpful not only for constructing an argument, but they also provide an excellent test of the cogency of someone else's argument. Any sound argument should satisfactorily answer each of the following four questions (unless one or more of these is granted, assumed, conceded or admitted by all parties):

First, is there a *need* for the proposed change?

Second, will the proposal *meet the need?*

Third, is the proposal *feasible?*

Fourth, will the proposal bring about *new and worse evils?*

Let's run through a particular example. Someone argues that the church needs a new Sunday school building with fifteen to twenty rooms at the cost of $200,000. Everyone agrees that there is a need for the change. Second, everyone concedes that this particular proposal will meet the need. But the debate gets hung up on the next issue: is such a proposal feasible? The discussion finally reaches the point where both sides are agreed that the proposal is feasible only if they could get all of the members of the congregation to tithe, but "if," in this instance, is a very large word. Since it does not seem possible to get all of the members of the congregation to tithe, the proposal must be abandoned or modified. And so the argument for the new building flounders upon the test of feasibility. Another problem may be run all the way down to the fourth issue. A particular disease may be cured by a proposal to take certain steps that would cure the patient, but the result may be to cure him of that disease while crippling him for life. To adopt the proposal would be to bring about new or worse evils. The proposal tested in terms of its side effects must be abandoned. Frequently arguments that seem attractive otherwise will be scuttled by tests three or four.

HOW TO ARGUE

Remember, you are concerned not only to win the argument, but also to win the listener. So, attitude in argumentation is crucial. Later, more must be said about the importance of the *ethos* or image of the speaker in persuasion. But for now, let us consider some principles of sound argumentation. Never use weak arguments. It is better to have one strong argument than five arguments, four of which are weak. Jesus Christ never used a weak argument; and we should not do so in his name. Weak arguments give a handle to the opposition. You may be sure that the opposition will focus upon the weak arguments only and avoid entirely a strong argument, even though it may be totally convincing. There are no weak arguments in the Scriptures. Preaching, therefore, does not admit of weak arguments.

However, some arguments may seem more impressive or more evidently convincing than others. This raises the old primacy-recency question: should the strongest argument be introduced first or last? Apart from matters where the attitude of a hostile audience settles this question, which is more effective? Experimental studies have not yet shown that one order is superior to the other. It would seem that often the best order would be: strongest, strong, stronger. If the strongest argument is presented first to a friendly audience, then it may be repeated continually throughout the message. This will enable the preacher to relate other arguments to the strongest one which may become the argumentative theme. By constant reference to it, the strongest argument can be indelibly impressed on the mind of the hearer.[7] Whenever there is one leading argument in a sermon, this argument may be put into one short graphic unforgettable sentence like, "Don't sell the day to buy the hour," or "Bow now in faith or later by force." This kind of sentence put in concrete form becomes the rock in the snowball that gets the job done.

Clarity in argument is crucial. This has been mentioned earlier. Not only is clarity crucial for informative speeches, but also for persuasive speaking as well. Here is a list of words that each speaker should carefully distinguish. It would be well for him to look up the etymology and current usages of each. These words should be known and distinguished to lend clarity to one's thinking and speaking: fact, opinion, theory, hypothesis, presupposition, belief, evidence and proof.

---

[7]God continually used the principle of repetition in the Scriptures: cf. the repetitive use of the phrase, "They shall know that I am the Lord," throughout the prophecy of Ezekiel, and also the covenantal slogan that in its several variations always contains the words "your God, my people." This slogan occurs from Genesis to Revelation.

SUGGESTED PROJECTS
For Classroom or Study

In the Classroom

1. Using one of the topics chosen earlier (or some other), prepare a speech to establish or change a belief. Be able to justify the choice of this topic by your knowledge of the beliefs of your audience. Be sure that at least one-half of the group disagrees with your viewpoint.

2. Hand in a one-page outline exactly as you did before, at least two days before you will speak.

In the Study

In the spaces below, list scriptural references to biblical usage of each type of argument.

Analogy	Cause	Example	Sign	Other Notations

Chapter Five

PERSUASIVE PREACHING
II—PREACHING TO MOTIVATE

DEFINITION

Speaking to motivate reaches the culmination or peak of public speaking. All of the arts learned for the previous two types of speeches must be employed, plus a third element. Speaking to inform largely focuses upon factual content; the intent is to communicate new information to the mind. Speaking to convince presents evidence and reasoning that leads to conclusions and should influence belief. Speaking to motivate adds a psychological or emotional element in order to get listeners to act upon the information and the conclusions. It is important to understand that in motivational speaking nothing previously learned is left behind. Note the stress upon *addition*. Poor motivational speaking bypasses facts and reasoning and appeals directly to the emotions. But proper motivation operates *through* these two former channels and is based upon them.

First of all, good exposition is essential because lasting motivation always must be founded upon solid information. Problems and their solutions need to be stated clearly. A clear explanation of *what* action to take must be given first. Only then can motivation be meaningful. Secondly, good argumentation stresses the reasons *why* such action should be taken. Thus argumentation is essential to convince the listener that what you are asking him to do should be done because there is a need and this course of action provides God's answer to the need, or that it is the best feasible and logical solution deduced by solid reasoning based upon evidence from the Word of God. Exposition then reveals what to do while argumentation says why it must be done.

81

THE NEW ELEMENT

The third and new element that is peculiar to but not used exclusively in motivational speaking (all of these elements must be understood only as emphases within each of these types of speaking), is the emotional or pathetic (from the Greek word *pathos*) element. The speaker seeks to activate his audience to accomplish certain ends through arousing an emotional desire by psychological means. In informative speaking the stress is upon the *what,* in argumentation the stress falls on the *why,* but in motivational speaking the stress is upon the *want.*

The etymology of the word emotion is helpful. The word comes from the Latin *emovere,* which means to stir or to upset. Physically speaking, an emotion is the upsetting of the normal sympathetic bodily action causing the parasympathetic to take over. It is a keying up of the body for action. It is important, however, to distinguish between emotion in a broad and in a narrow sense. Emotion in the broadest sense includes what might be called *impulse* (or persuasion by the use of emotion alone). By impulse we mean the unreasoned acquiescence in an emotional drive. In contrast, emotional appeal in the narrower sense means acquiescence in emotion growing out of conclusions reached by solid reasoning from factual evidence. Thus the emotional element recommended here is the acceptance of an emotional drive only after reasoned judgment.

THE USE OF THE NARRATIVE

Narratives often may be used very effectively in conjunction with all three types of preaching. They may be used in exposition and argument to clarify and illustrate, or as examples. But the narrative is particularly useful as an agent for conveying emotion. A good narrative by definition carries a great deal of emotion with it, as we have seen in the discussion of the delivery of narratives. The introduction of complication, growing suspense and climax is in itself the introduction of emotional factors. Thus one good way of introducing emotional appeal as the new element in motivational speaking is through the use of narratives.

EFFECTIVE USE OF EMOTIONAL APPEAL

There are several factors involved in the effective use of psychological or emotional appeal. First, audience analysis is essential. Speakers must know what motivates audiences in general and each audience in particular. Paul was able to toss the golden apple between the Pharisees and the Sadducees by raising the issue of the resurrection, because he knew his audience. As Luke says:

> "But perceiving that one party were Sadducees and the other Pharisees, Paul began crying out in the Council, Brethren, I am a Pharisee, a son of Pharisees; I am on trial for the hope and resurrection of the dead!"[1]

What motivates one audience may not motivate another. Hopefully that which motivates a conservative congregation will be different from that which motivates the Mafia. What this means is that the speaker must be clear about the motive or motives to which he appeals. He must be able to state these motives exactly. In other words, he must be able to give a reasoned, ethical, biblical case for arousing these particular emotions.

MOTIVATION RESEARCH

Secondly, the discussion of audience analysis leads to the question of motivation research, which has been a large factor in modern advertising. Motivation research is the study of the psychology of human motivation. The beating that once was given to Wall Street now is received by Madison Avenue, or as it more affectionately has been called, Mad Avenue. Motiva-

---

[1] Acts 23:6. Note the word "perceive." By underscoring this fact, Luke points out Paul's conscious use of audience analysis.

tion researchers have discovered that sinful man operates on an emotional basis far more than he recognizes. (The Bible has been saying this for centuries.) This, they say, is partly true because of basic irrational desires and needs like status, sex and security. Hence, the policy of motivational researchers is to sell more than the product and service. They want to appeal directly to these irrational desires. The motivational researcher, therefore, will insist that his client sell, in addition to the product and service, the promise of the fulfillment of a basic desire (or, better still, desires). It is in order to fulfil these desires, they say, that man acts. Motivational researchers have illustrated by interesting data the old biblical facts about sinful human beings.[2] For example, the eye rate blink of women in grocery stores has been shown to be the same as that of persons who are hypnotized.[3] Hence, they buy under suggestion. Homes are no longer thought of as houses. The home is used to appeal to a woman as an expression of herself, an extension of her personality. To men, the home is said to symbolize mother; a place of calm refuge.[4] Stores must no longer sell shoes; instead, they must sell lovely feet. For a long while, of course, people had been saying, you don't sell the steak, you sell the sizzle. Take the soft drink industry, for example. Pepsi Cola launched an advertising campaign several years ago that clearly illustrates the motivational approach. Pepsi's advertising on television and radio was quite blatant. Such commercials as the following were drummed into our ears day after day: "Do you know you can buy sociability in a bottle?" Then followed the sound of a sweet young voice singing, "Be young and fair and debonair, be sociable—buy Pepsi." Pepsi sales soared so high and cut so deeply into

---

[2]Cf. especially, II Peter 2:10-14; Titus 1:10-12, and many other parallel passages.

[3]Vance Packard, *The Hidden Persuaders,* Pocket Books, Inc., N. Y.: 1958, p. 91, 92.

[4]*Ibid.,* p. 79.

Coke that Coke had to respond with a similar appeal. Their reply was, "Things go better with Coke." Coke will help you to solve all of life's problems. Packard, in his book *Hidden Persuaders*, tells the interesting story of a manufacturer who packaged the same soap in yellow boxes and in blue boxes. When the soap was tested, women said that the soap in the yellow boxes was too strong. They said that the soap in the blue boxes left the clothes dirty looking. The manufacturer finally settled on a third box colored blue with splashes of yellow,[5] because after testing it the women declared that the soap in it was magnificent. This was, of course, exactly the same product that previously had been declared too strong or too weak.

ETHICAL QUESTIONS

It is impossible to avoid the use of emotional appeal, as George Campbell recognized in 1719:

"To say that it is possible to persuade without speaking to the passions is but at best a kind of specious nonsense. . . . This he cannot avoid doing if he speak to the purpose."[6]

Long before the motivational research fad, Campbell knew what every good Christian speaker recognizes, that the problem is really not whether we will use emotional appeal, but whether we will use it well and ethically (that is, in accordance with the biblical ethic). Preachers are whole persons speaking to whole persons. Broadus says, "The ignorant use emotional appeal too much, while the cultured use it too little."[7] Perhaps the real problem is that the ignorant and unscrupulous cultivate psychological or emotional appeal to

---

[5]*Ibid.*, p. 11.

[6]George Campbell, *A Philosophy of Oratory*, Bk. I, ch. 7, par. 4.

[7]John Broadus, *The Preparation and Delivery of Sermons*, Smith, English and Company, Philadelphia: 1875, p. 235.

the neglect of logical appeal, while the cultured[8] and ethical
tend to cultivate logical appeal to the neglect of the psychological. The real point here is that Christian speakers ought to
cultivate both. Preachers must keep both in proper balance
and in proper relationship to the particular purpose of the
sermon.

Vance Packard and Ernest Dichter perhaps have best set
forth the two extremes with respect to the use of emotional
appeal. Their exchange raised many of the pertinent ethical issues involved so that a critique of these positions is helpful to
the Christian who wants to use emotion properly in speaking.
The thesis of Vance Packard's *Hidden Persuaders* might be
summarized by his negative answer to the question: "Have we
any right to manipulate people into buying or doing what we
want when they have no idea what is going on?" Dichter set
forth three major propositions in his book, *The Strategy of
Desire* (Dichter's answer to Packard's book): First, ethics is
changeable, relative and fluid. The new understanding of motivation that we have today requires a brand new ethics based
upon it. We now know man's basic needs for security, sex,
status, etc., and recognize that these needs must be satisfied
for him to enjoy a full and integrated life. Secondly, Dichter
claims that rationality is the fetish of the 20th Century mind.
Our society, he says, will not allow us to admit man's true irrationality. The motivational research approach, therefore,
simply covers up (sugar-coats) this irrational base for action
with rationalization. Thirdly, Dichter strongly advocates a
new hedonism. He says that hedonism must be made respect-
able in order that men may live the full life. Strictly speaking,
he claims, products and services are incidental; it is the fulfillment of life's basic desires that counts. As a matter of fact,
that is not even strictly true, for it is not their actual fulfillment that matters, but rather the fact that we *think* they

---

[8]Here I use Broadus' term merely by accommodation, not because I
accept it.

have been fulfilled. Therefore, if Pepsi does not really deliver on its claim for sociability, that is fine if you *think* you are more sociable and thereby become a better adjusted person with a fuller life. The crux of all this is that the end justifies the means. So on the one hand Packard's view is that every use of emotional appeal should be made known to the listener to avoid manipulating him unfairly and unjustly. Dichter, on the other hand, maintains that the end justifies the means.

The Christian must avoid both of these extremes. Packard's approach goes too far in the one direction. Every use of emotional appeal simply cannot be tagged and labeled as such in a speech. Every word uttered carries some emotion. Even those passages of a sermon that seemingly are not very heavily charged emotionally, *may* be for *some*. Some persons may consider terms, phrases, references or statements highly emotional because of their personal understanding of them or because of special problems that they associate with these comments. Thus Packard's solution vitiates the personality of man as God has made him and must be rejected out of hand. Packard's plea rightly alarms us and makes us take account of the gross amount of manipulation that is taking place. Nevertheless he goes too far in his proposed solution to the problem. Dichter's dictum that the end justifies the means boils down to this: that ethics applies to goals and not to means. Therefore, the only really debatable factor is the goal. This proposition totally ignores the command, "Thou shalt not bear false witness." Moreover, his goal of a full hedonistic life runs directly contrary to the biblical admonition, "Seek ye first the kingdom of God and . . . all these things will be added unto you." Dichter is also wrong in over-stressing the irrationality of man. Though in a world of sin, men do act irrationally, and though Dichter has contributed to our understanding of this aspect of man, his solution, it must be observed, is sinfully irrational, as it appeals not to the objective revelation of God, but to the warped nature of sinful man.

A biblical approach, of course, begins with the Scriptures,

the Word of God, as the standard of faith and practice. According to the Bible, God made man with reason *and* with emotion. The whole man must act, and thus the whole man must be reached. Reason should not be bypassed in reaching emotions; the logical dimension must not be *replaced* by the psychological. The solution, therefore, will not come in an either/or form. It is wrong to *substitute* emotion for facts, evidence and argumentation, but it is equally wrong to *substitute* logical for psychological methods. A preacher must not write in the margin of the sermon, "Yell loudly here, argument weak." Nor may he speak about heaven or hell dispassionately. He must not misrepresent the cross by preaching it only didactically and not also doxologically. Sermons must have exclamation points! The Christian preacher, therefore, must present a biblically defensible case for all action, *together with* the use of appropriate emotional appeal. The Chrisrian preaches the sizzle *and* the steak, not the sizzle *instead* of the steak, or the steak *without* the sizzle. The Christian in preaching (or when engaging in any other form of speaking) makes promises or raises hopes only when he knows (because God has said so) that these will materialize. As a matter of fact, the Christian message alone lives up to its claim; the Christian message alone can deliver on the promises that are made. Christians may, therefore, rightly appeal to all of the God-given desires of man, for Christianity can be demonstrated scripturally to meet every psychological need. However, the appeal must not be to any abuse of a psychological drive, but always must be made in terms of the scripturally revealed commandment for the proper use or fulfillment of that drive. Christians, therefore, ought to be using emotional appeal with more confidence and more fully than anyone. As Campbell put it, "So far from being an unfair mode of persuasion to move the passions . . . there is no persuasion without moving them."[9]

---

[9]*Op. cit.*, Bk. I, Ch. 7, par. 4. Note such passages as II Peter 1:13, 3:1

THE LANGUAGE OF EMOTIONAL APPEAL

Emotional language is more highly colored, emotionally charged, and strongly connotative than didactic language. The use of words must be governed by the biblical ethic of truth. Probably nowhere else can one go wrong as easily as in the choice of language. Words can be subtly *slanted.* Unfair connotations may be added or important connotations may be subtracted. For instance, euphemisms often have been substituted for what some have considered difficult doctrines of the Scriptures. Sin has frequently been called error or failure when the context called for nothing less than the strongest words available to designate or describe a violation of the law of a holy God. Here are some examples of the differences that can be made by substituting emotionally charged words for other words. For instance, the same woman might be called either a mother (think of the warm connotations surrounding that word) or mother-in-law! The very same slice of meat may be labeled either "filet mignon" or called "a first-rate piece of dead cow." The airlines long ago learned the importance of euphemism. This is seen clearly in the evolution of the language used on what somewhat euphemistically might be called the chuckbag. Years ago, the words printed on this small but essential item found in the pocket in front of each seat used to read "for vomiting." Probably more people vomited as a result of this highly suggestive language than because of nausea due to air movement. Then this phraseology was euphemised to "for air sickness." Later on it became, more euphemistically, "for motion discomfort." And in more recent times the bag has either been left completely blank, or ticktacktoe and other games have been printed on the side. So

---

where *diegeiro,* "to stir up" or "excite the emotions," is used. Here Peter plainly reveals his purpose. He wants to arouse emotional responses to the intellectual facts learned previously. Cf. also Hebrews 10:24 where the writer speaks of "stimulating" one another to good works. The word used here *(parozuno)* is a term associated with strong emotional excitement.

the importance of the careful and accurate use of language and of thinking through the exact connotations of emotionally charged terms is essential to good ethical motivational preaching.

THE SALESMEN'S CLOSE

The salesmen for years have been known to be experts in motivation. Their livelihood depends upon it. Many practices that are used to motivate customers (such as dropping the pencil on the floor so that the customer picks it up and, therefore, has it in his hand ready to sign the contract) of course cannot be recommended for motivational speaking. However, there is much to learn from the salesman. Perhaps as crucial a matter as any is learning how to close. The *close* is the conclusion to the salesman's pitch. The question is studied carefully by every good salesman because everything depends upon whether at that point he is able to get the customer to buy. No matter how well he has done in presenting information conclusively and convincingly throughout the salestalk, if in the conclusion he fails to motivate the customer, he fails. If a congregation is convinced but fails to take action, the preacher also has *failed*. The problem in conservative (and particularly in Reformed churches) is that while preachers do instruct and do convince people, they do not know how to move them to action. Often this is the result of improper closing. Congregations may become concerned, even anxious to do something about a problem, yet they do not know *what* to do or *how* to go about doing it. Sermons often are not specific enough. Instead of urging believers to pray, why not urge them to come to prayer meeting Wednesday night and pray for . . . (then spell out several specific needs)? Instead of merely saying, "*Study* your Bible," why not also make Bible study guides available in the vestibule?

Remember, too, that it is easy for people to forget. Other interests intervene when they leave the church service, and if they have nothing to carry with them, they may easily forget even their best Sunday resolutions before Tuesday. Moreover, they don't know what to do, or how to do it, because we seldom tell them what to do or how to do it. The genius of a good close consists in presenting concrete action that can be taken *now;* it consists in striking while the iron is hot. There should be in the conclusion of a speech to move to action a direct appeal to do something that the listener can reasonably be expected to do. This involves usually: providing or pointing out certain ways and means that make it feasible for the believer to follow now. Gasoline companies encourage driving by distributing maps. Preachers need to learn how to give directions as well as to urge people to take trips. For instance, if the sermon has to do with Bible study and the listener has been encouraged to begin a study in a particular book of the Bible which will be conducted throughout the next six weeks, taking a certain number of chapters or verses at a time, he might go away from church with a pamphlet that the usher handed him at the door as he was leaving which would contain a mimeographed six-week program for such a Bible study. Following the service perhaps a pocket portion of the Bible book also might be distributed. Members often are enabled to begin and to continue new biblical courses of action as a result. Such help conserves good desires and determinations which otherwise might fall on stoney ground. Often simply pointing out the first step, or in other cases laying out a step-by-step process as a possible way of obeying God's Word, will make a tremendous difference.

The end of a motivational speech, like the end of a sharp pencil, should come to a point. It should answer the question, "Where do I go from here?" The speaker should have his specific purpose so well in mind that he can state it in a one-word imperative, and it is often wise to do so in the conclusion. He may say Investigate! Study! Go! Write! Witness! One way to check your conclusion is to read the purpose statement that you placed at the top of the page, then skip over the rest of the outline and look directly at the conclusion. Do they correspond? Does your conclusion urge the same action that you set out to urge? If it does not, there may be something wrong with the conclusion itself, or there may be something wrong in the body of the speech. It may be that at some point in the body, the speech takes a turn so that your conclusion ends at a different goal than the one toward which you started out. Thus the comparison of the initial purpose statement with the conclusion provides a very important check on the whole speech.

THE SPEAKER'S PSYCHOLOGICAL IMAGE

So far, we have discussed *evidence* and its use in persuasion. Such logical considerations largely have to do with *content*. We have also discussed emotion, which primarily has to do with the *audience*. But we have said nothing about the ethical side of preaching.[10] *Ethos* has to do with the *speaker*. The psychology of motivation not only has implications about outlining and style, but where the P and A (preacher and audience) lines in the homogeneous grid meet there is significant interaction. The personality of the speaker, therefore, is essential to consider in motivational preaching.

In the Goldwater campaign, for example, the press built an extremely unfavorable image for Goldwater which doubtless had much to do with his landslide defeat. In accordance with the philosophy of motivation based upon a biblical ethic derived from the Ten Commandments, the preacher should be concerned to build a favorable image that honestly fits his own personality. In other words, he must not build up a false image. Such an image is an image only. It is like claiming that sociability can be bought in a bottle. The image must be true to the facts. This was precisely the fault of the Pharisees, whom Christ denounced as "hypocrites" (cf. Matt. 23). The Christian preacher needs to "take heed to himself" as well as

---

[10]Here "ethical" is used in its classical rhetorical sense: *ethos* meaning the personal, psychological image of the speaker.

the preacher's prestige or general repu- of what position he holds in his field, in that his reputation is nationally, and what consists of his experiences, his knowledge, associations, his titles; in sum, the authority goes before him. Remember the taunts of who scoffed about him as a mere "car- also John 6:42; 7:15, 28-29), and even more sympathetic asked, "Can any good Nazareth?" (John 1:46).

reputation about the preacher's character part in what people will think of him, why II Corinthians was written. Paul spends ce in defending himself from attacks against because he cared about his own reputation cause the attack against his character was an is message. Anyone who has read II Corinthi- nnot fail to see how closely authority, charac- ge are related. (Incidentally, II Corinthians in a modern translation since the King James this book is extremely poor.) And finally, im- knowledge an general ability in the field about speak. Sometimes it is crucial just to say, "I was Cor. 15:5-8). Many people are tired of slick ad- niques and have begun to ask: "Is the speaker m within his own element?" They are disgusted yers on television to recommend brand X razor y reason, rightly, "Why do ball players know more es than I?" Liberal achers who, while decrying ity of the Scriptures made themselves out to political and econo authorities, have begun to essure of just such man backlash.

The Preacher's Prt Image. The present image hat the audience ives from seeing and hear- immediately e, during and after the deliv- n. His appce, consisting largely of his

to his
(I Tim.
image)
Christian
means th
of a godly

A study
portance o
ity. At Nor
played for t
mental subje
person had de
was identified
that he was th
States; and the
student. I do no
periment, but w
trated that what
crucial significanc
non-acceptance of
his image. The hig
ceptance than the
toward the ideas of
attitude toward the
actually the same.[12]
Paul's exhortation to
portance, part of whic

But what, precisely,
ethical appeal (image)
least two things:
First, *The Preacher's*

spective image refer
tation. This consists
his denomination, w
it is locally. It also
his degrees, his asso
(or lack of it) that
Christ's adversaries
penter's son" (see
those who were
thing come out of

In addition, th
plays an importa
This is one reason
a good bit of sp
his character, no
in itself, but be
attack against h
ans carefully ca
ter and messa
should be read
translation of
age rates his
which he will
there" (cf. I
vertising tec
speaking fr
with ball pl
blades. The
about blad
the author
be social
feel th

---

[11]The importance of com
ers cannot be overstressed.
[12]E. C. Buehler and Wil ug
and Row, N. Y.: 1962, p. 66

to his doctrine *so that* his "progress may be evident to all" (I Tim. 4:15, 16). The preacher's manifest personality (or image) should closely approximate his inner personality. Christians should strive for the image of a reality; and that means that for his image to be effective, it must be the image of a godly and competent man.[11]

A study cited by Buehler and Linkugel illustrates the importance of reputation and association to a speaker's credibility. At Northwestern University the same taped speech was played for three different audiences. In each case the experimental subjects were told that an entirely different kind of person had delivered the speech. To one audience the speaker was identified as a high government official; another was told that he was the head of the Communist Party in the United States; and the third was led to believe that he was a fellow student. I do not want to comment on the ethics of the experiment, but wish only to note that the study clearly illustrated that what the audience thought of the speaker was of crucial significance. The study showed that the acceptance or non-acceptance of what he had to say was dependent upon his image. The high government official got much wider acceptance than the other two. There was a negative response toward the ideas of the Communist and a who-could-care-less attitude toward the thoughts of a peer. Yet the ideas were actually the same.[12] Preachers, therefore, must recognize that Paul's exhortation to "take heed" to one's self is of great importance, part of which has to do with his ethical appeal.

But what, precisely, is one's image? When we speak of the ethical appeal (image) of the speaker, we are talking about at least two things:

First, *The Preacher's Prospective Image.* The words pro-

---

[11]The importance of continued self evaluation before God and others cannot be overstressed.

[12]E. C. Buehler and Wil A. Linkugel, *Speech: A First Course,* Harper and Row, N. Y.: 1962, p. 66.

spective image refer to the preacher's prestige or general reputation. This consists of what position he holds in his field, in his denomination, what his reputation is nationally, and what it is locally. It also consists of his experiences, his knowledge, his degrees, his associations, his titles; in sum, the authority (or lack of it) that goes before him. Remember the taunts of Christ's adversaries who scoffed about him as a mere "carpenter's son" (see also John 6:42; 7:15, 28-29), and even those who were more sympathetic asked, "Can any good thing come out of Nazareth?" (John 1:46).

In addition, the reputation about the preacher's character plays an important part in what people will think of him. This is one reason why II Corinthians was written. Paul spends a good bit of space in defending himself from attacks against his character, not because he cared about his own reputation in itself, but because the attack against his character was an attack against his message. Anyone who has read II Corinthians carefully cannot fail to see how closely authority, character and message are related. (Incidentally, II Corinthians should be read in a modern translation since the King James translation of this book is extremely poor.) And finally, image rates his knowledge and general ability in the field about which he will speak. Sometimes it is crucial just to say, "I was there" (cf. I Cor. 15:5-8). Many people are tired of slick advertising techniques and have begun to ask: "Is the speaker speaking from within his own element?" They are disgusted with ball players on television who recommend brand X razor blades. They reason, rightly, "Why do ball players know more about blades than I?" Liberal preachers who, while decrying the authority of the Scriptures, have made themselves out to be social, political and economic authorities, have begun to feel the pressure of just such a layman backlash.

Second, *The Preacher's Present Image.* The present image is the image that the audience receives from seeing and hearing the speaker immediately before, during and after the delivery of his sermon. His appearance, consisting largely of his grooming and confidence (poise), his voice, his body, and his language, his pronunciation and grammar, are external, but important, factors that determine image. Also, image is shaped by the content of the sermon, its organization and the reasoning behind the argument. It consists of the attitudes that the audience thinks (though they may be led astray when the image is false[13]) that he has toward them and toward his subject matter. If he seems to be noncommittal toward his subject or apathetic or enthusiastic, this makes a tremendous difference. If he seems to have the welfare and concern of the audience at heart, he gets a different reception than when he simply seems to be putting in time. His approach (whether it is a hard or soft sell) can be fundamental. His basic personal integrity and sincerity, as well as the persons and causes with which he identifies himself as he speaks, all help build his image.[14] All of these factors have a lot to do with the present image. Yet that image is not static; it often grows and changes during the sermon. It is important for a speaker to think about these matters because they are so vitally related to the audience's receptivity. The message is crucial, not the preacher's reputation; but more often than not listeners too closely associate the two. There are two kinds of image power that speakers possess. Either consciously or unconcsiously, audiences recognize these. First, there is what the Scriptures call *dunamis* (the Greek word for that sort of internal power or authority that stems from the man as a personality in his own right). This is the word consistently (though not exclusively) associated with miracles; they are called "powers" (cf. Acts 2:22, 10:38; 1:8). Over against this is *exousia* (externally-conferred power). This authority, Christ also possessed: cf.

---

[13]The image may be false negatively as well as positively. A preacher may have warm feelings internally that do not constitute part of his image. The audience may misinterpret his stiff, formal image for coldness toward them and their needs.

[14]Cf. Acts 4:13

Luke 5:24; Matthew 18:18. It is significant to notice that this authority was recognized (Luke 4:32).

To sum up, emotional persuasion has to do with the audience and the speaker in a more intimate relationship with each other. The Christian minister, therefore, must strive to be a godly and competent man, for the sake of the gospel.

SUGGESTED PROJECTS
For Classroom or Study

In the Classroom

1. Prepare a speech designed to motivate your audience to take some action you believe it would be reasonable to expect them to take, assuming your speech will be effective. Strike while the iron is hot. Plan to call upon your group to take some specific action. You may want to pass the hat to collect for a cause, pass around a paper for the signature of those who will give blood, distribute a mimeographed prayer list, etc. But whatever you do, urge the group to take concrete action, and provide the ways and means for them to do so.

2. Be sure to hand in an outline at least two days before, prepared according to previous specifications.

3. In this speech, be very careful about the connotations of the emotionally freighted words that you may use. In most of these speeches you will want to use a narrative and some examples.

4. Imagine several radically different congregations, and in one short paragraph write out the prospective image each would have of you.

In the Study

1. Ask yourself, your wife, your children, your elders and anyone else who may know, what image your congregation has of you.

2. Prepare a motivational sermon and plan to follow through with concrete action that will help your congregation to respond. For instance, if you speak on the importance of Bible study, be prepared also to announce a six week's course on *Basic Principles of Bible Interpretation,* have the ushers hand out a brochure on *Methods of Effective Bible Study* in the narthex, etc.

Chapter Six

ORGANIZING CONTENT FOR DELIVERY

ORGANIZATION IS IMPORTANT

Organization, as the word implies, has to do with how the parts of a speech or sermon are put together to form a unified whole. Students often give less care and attention to organization than they should, with the result that presbyteries and congregations are unhappy with the noticeable deficiencies that accompany this failure. You can hardly blame them, since it is good organization that largely enables the listener to grasp scriptural truth systematically. It is also good organization that makes biblical teaching memorable. And it is good organization that gives force to the logical and psychological impact of an argument. Poor organization, on the other hand, can distort meaning, weaken arguments, make the Christian message seem foolish, and turn off his audience before a speaker has reached the second point. You can understand, then, why it is important for you to take time to learn how to plan a sermon properly.

THE PREACHING TEXT AND ORGANIZATION

In preaching, the text itself may help determine the organization of the sermon. Many passages lend themselves to a given structure. The use of antithesis in Proverbs and Psalms and in much of John's writings naturally suggests an antithetical or two-point sermon.[1] Sometimes structure is in dispute and organization may depend upon the resolution of an exegetical or textual problem. For example, a study of Jude 22, 23 raises the textual question as to whether Jude is speaking about two or three distinct groups. If there are two, then the sermon involves two attitudes toward two groups, but if there

---

[1] For instance, compare Proverbs 12:15-28. Note especially verses 15 and 28.

98

are three, it requires three attitudes toward three different classes of people. The structure of a sermon on the passage doubtless would be affected strongly by the resolution of the problem.

While the text itself may afford the natural divisions for a sermon, this is not necessarily the way to structure a sermon. As a matter of fact, not one sermon recorded in the New Testament is organized along the structural lines of an Old Testament writers frequently used an amanuensis) are others. The preacher must learn to translate poetic, narrative or apocalyp-oriented to the speaking situation. It is essential, however, during the preparation of the message to carefully analyze the text itself, looking at its divisions and possibly outlining it in detail. But an outline representing the structure of the scriptural passage may be quite different from the outline from which you will preach on Sunday morning. Failure to recognize this has been a frequent cause for failure in preaching. In planning a sermon it is of great importance to determine the type of biblical literature from which the text comes. Rhetorical analysis of the passage is fundamental to proper outlining. Preaching is one biblical structural form; poetry is another. Apocalyptic form, narrative form, and epistolary form (though this is close to speaking for a preacher, because New Testament writers frequently used amanuensis) are others. The preacher must learn to translate poetic, narrative or apocalyptic forms into a preaching form. An outline that is good for poetry or good for narratives may not be good for preaching, and particularly may not be suited to the particular audience to whom this message is to be preached.

In outlining, then, it is not the division of the text but the content, the purpose and the audience that first must be taken into account. Preachers must learn to translate other structural forms into a rhetorical or preaching form. When doing so, purpose becomes the controlling factor. For example, a Proverb capsulizes a tremendous slice of life in a pithy epigrammatic sentence. The preacher may, and indeed must, enlarge upon this thought as it applies to a variety of circumstances. It must not be the natural divisions of the text that determine the outline, but rather the subject matter. Other factors, such as audience and purpose, also must be taken into consideration. A consideration of purpose automatically takes the preaching situation and the audience into account. The question boils down to this. *What* does the Holy Spirit in this text intend to *do,* to *whom, when,* and for *what* reasons? Speaking in terms of audience analysis, the outline may be inductive or deductive. There is a great psychological difference between the two. Before deciding upon the basic approach in the outline, a preacher should learn all he can about the audience's knowledge and attitude toward himself and toward his subject. So, while he must preach Christ from his text, the preacher must determine whether he may use the divisions natural to the text itself, or whether he will need to translate these into a preaching form adapted to the audience and occasion.

In addition to audience analysis, the preacher needs to learn whether the intention of the writer in the passage was to inform, convince, or motivate. If the text is largely informative, the preacher's purpose is clarity, understanding, and retention. This will require bold visible structure. The outline must fit the purpose. The preacher may make use of enumeration. Convincing involves an outline with less obvious structure. Logical relationships and progression, rather than divisions, should stand out, though these may take form as points and transitions. Motivational speech requires the least obvious outlines, even though behind the motivational sermon the structure is as firm as for informative speaking. The difference is not in whether the outline is as clear and definite; the difference has to do with how strongly the outline needs to be stressed (as such) to the audience.

PARTS OF THE OUTLINE

Outlines should contain a minimum of five distinct parts:

1. The Title
2. A statement of the Specific Purpose (theme or Central Idea).
3. The Introduction.
4. The Body (consisting of the Major and Minor points (subpoints), illustrative material, Scripture or other references, and transitional sentences.
5. The Conclusion.

Much has been said about Specific Purpose, Introductions and Conclusions elsewhere. Therefore, in this chapter we will refer largely to the organization and outlining of the Body of the Sermon. But first, let us say a brief word about titles.

Blackwood took time to study the practice of newspaper journalists, and discovered that as a rule editors take pains to see that "a line of newspaper publicity" contains no more than "four strong words."[2] Sensationalism ought to be avoided and titles should not make promises on which you do not intend to deliver.[3] Titles may be used to identify a topic, arouse interest in the topic, or create suspense about the topic.

ORGANIZING THE BODY

One way to begin organizing the body of the sermon is to write down all of the points you wish to make, each on a separate 3" x 5" card. Then sort out the major (coordinate) points from the minor (subordinate) points and arrange these in outline form. You may wish to rearrange them several times; cards allow for maximum flexibility in doing so. The divisions of the subject (purpose or theme) are the major

---

[2] Andrew W. Blackwood, *The Preparation of Sermons,* Abingdon Press, N. Y.: 1958, p. 94. By "strong words," Blackwood means nouns, verbs, adverbs and adjectives.

[3] Titles can be lies; such lies infuriate persons who visit especially to listen to a sermon on an announced topic only to discover that the topic was used merely as bait or as a springboard.

points. Be sure that they are mutually exclusive. That is, they cannot overlap or cover the same territory. Ordinarily these should be limited to a maximum number of four or five. That is about all that a congregation can remember. When you have more than this, probably a second sermon on the subject is indicated. The divisions of the major points that explain or support them are the minor (subordinate) points. These divisions of the major points must also be coordinate to one another. Since minor points must coordinate too, therefore, they also must be mutually exclusive. Putting each point on a separate card allows you to group them in various ways until you finalize the correct relationships between them.

In much the same way that one fits together the pieces of a jigsaw puzzle, the points on the cards may be grouped, all the greens, the blues, the reds, etc., to see which ideas fit together. You will find that this method also makes it easy to sift out the extraneous materials. There should be more material than you can use if you have done your work well. These "extra" cards may be filed for future use. You will probably end up with somewhere between two and four major points, plus two to four minor points for each of these. The major points should be stated in parallel form and in terms that directly involve the audience. You are not merely stating a doctrine or reporting a past event; you are preaching God's Word to a living congregation. Thus sentences like: "I. Evangelism is the work of the whole church (Acts 8:4)" or "I. Everyone in the early church evangelized" should read instead: "God calls every one of *you* to evangelize." Then, in the minor points the biblical basis for this contemporary call may be explained: "A. It was not merely the Apostles who evangelized, Acts 8: 1, 4." In this way, the present relevance of the Word of God is clearly set forth. Every sermon should contain a contemporary call growing from a biblical basis.

The sentence structure of every outline ought to be complete with a capital at the beginning and a period at the end. In other words, full sentences should be used for each point.

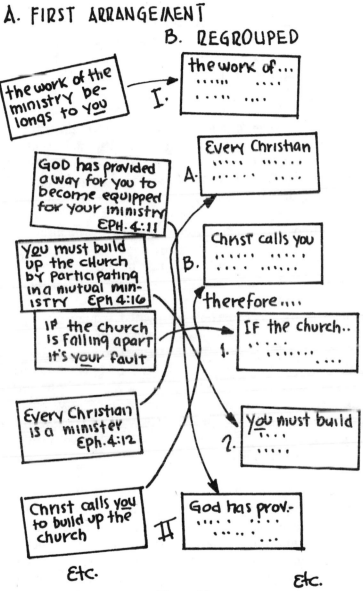

Figure 11
Outlining by Grouping and Regrouping

This is crucial for filing and future reference, as well as for precision. Finally, you must determine the order of both the major and the minor points. Where a logical or chronological order is not required, other factors, such as the primacy-recency question (a matter of psychological order) may arise.

TYPES OF OUTLINES

Outlines of sermons and speeches to inform most frequently use one or more of the following patterns: classification and division, time order, space order, comparison and contrast and definition. Outlines of speeches to convince may include problem-solution, effect to cause, and cause to effect patterns. The validity of each point in these may be tested by adding the words *since* or *because* to any of the minor points to see if they really do support the major point to which they are subordinate. The same test may be applied to the major divisions to determine whether they support the theme (or central idea of the talk). In speeches to motivate, one form frequently used is Monroe's motivated sequence. The form includes the following in this sequence: attention, need, solution, visualization, and appeal. These five elements are used in this way: 1. Ladies, 2. do you suffer from dishpan hands? 3. If so, use Sudsy. 4. In four days your hands will be soft and look lovely. 5. Next time you shop pick up Sudsy. This is obviously the commercial format. It is well worth knowing because it is the way that people in our time have been conditioned to receive appeals to action.

To test whether you are clear about your specific purpose (or theme) in a motivational sermon, you may sum it up in a one-word imperative. If your organization lacks unity you will find this difficult to do. If you do not have one central thrust, you will confuse your congregation. The outline should serve the specific purpose (theme) of the sermon. Its structure is, therefore, thematically or telically conditioned. The sermon is a thematic design. To understand whether you know clearly what you want your audience to do, force yourself to sum up your message in *one* word, like "Pray! Work! Repent! Go! Believe! Investigate! Read!" Transitions are often of great importance (especially in sermons to convince) and are, therefore, worth noting in outlines. Spell them out in the outline itself. Similarities (cf. Greek *men . . . de*) or differences (cf. Greek *alla*) between two elements that need to be bridged can become the means of transition. You may stress logical relationships (cf. Greek *oun*) as well

USE FULL SENTENCES

Full sentence outlines have been required for this course rather than skeleton outlines. There are several reasons for this. The first, and least important, is so that the instructor may be able to understand what you have written; mere phrases and words may be very meaningful to you, but may be totally unintelligible to someone else. But of greater importance is the fact that what is perfectly clear to you today may not be quite so clear in five years when you may wish to modify and use the outline again. At the time of composition, it might seem that you could never forget the ideas behind a phrase or word that seems so vivid now, yet you will! Take the word of someone who learned the hard way (and the word of many others in the ministry who agree). Another important reason for using a full sentence outline is that it allows you to preserve all the work you have done *in one place.* Instead of preserving worksheets *and* an outline, you can file all the results on one looseleaf notebook page. Finally, consider the fact that when you determine to write full sentences rather than the mere jottings, you put yourself under greater obligation to make sense. It is too easy to delude yourself into believing that you understand what you are going to say (when you don't) if you do not force yourself to make sense on paper. Sentences demand more precision and accuracy than phrases or words, and thus provide one antidote to fuzziness.[4]

---

[4]This rule by no means excludes the use of abbreviations or the

OTHER PRACTICAL TIPS

Using a pen, rather than a typewriter, assures maximum flexibility in outlining. Instead of composing two outlines, as some do (a bare skeleton for use at the time of delivery and a fuller outline for storage), you may put both on one page by simply lettering the "preaching outline" in larger letters.[5] Using the new highlighting colored marking pens, you can further identify main heads, illustrations, Scripture references, etc., by coding each with a distinct color. When your eye drops down on a page set up like this, you can hardly miss picking up the cue you need immediately. Compare the following:

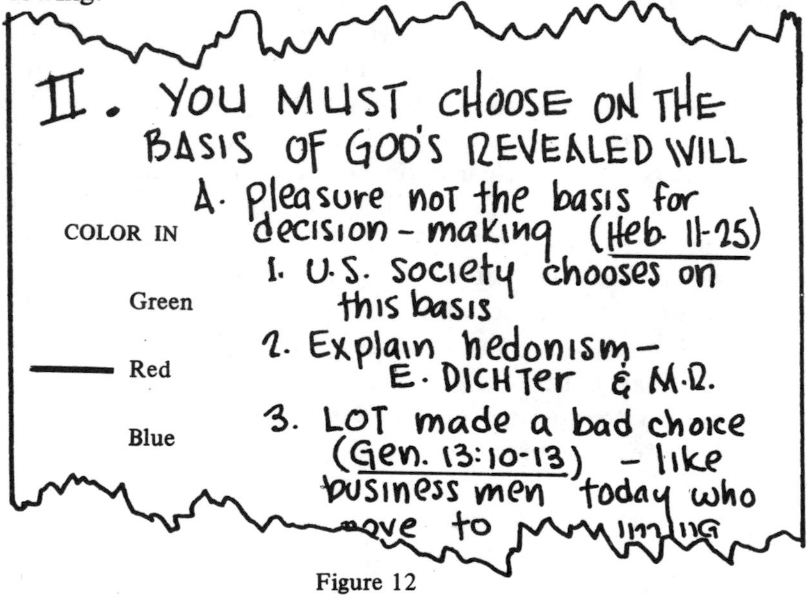

Figure 12
Coding Outline in Color

COLOR IN

Green

—— Red

Blue

II. YOU MUST CHOOSE ON THE BASIS OF GOD'S REVEALED WILL
A. Pleasure not the basis for decision-making (Heb. 11-25)
  1. U.S. society chooses on this basis
  2. Explain hedonism— E. DICHTer & M.R.
  3. LOT made a bad choice (Gen. 13:10-13) — like business men today who move to...

omission of words in a sentence that does not obscure meaning because they are obvious. For instance, to conserve space the previous sentence might be written as follows: "Rule doesn't exclude abbrev's or omission of wds. that doesn't obscure because obvious."

[5] And just in case you should forget some detail, you will always have it in the pulpit with you.

This full outline may be filed in a looseleaf notebook (probably the 10" x 7" notebook is most useful) according to whatever filing method you develop. Probably you will want to begin with at least three or four notebooks:

1. Old Testament notebook
2. New Testament notebook
3. Doctrinal and Occasional notebook
4. Preaching notebook

The fourth is a handy separate notebook that you may wish to take into the pulpit with you. If a sermon is secured in a looseleaf notebook, then it will not go sailing off the pulpit with a sudden gust of wind or the sweep of a hand.

Organization is vital and you must pay close attention to it. You will need practice. One practical way of practicing is to follow the rule of taking down all of your classnotes and reading notes in outline form while at seminary.[6] If the lecturer speaks too rapidly, do your best at the time, then when you go home, reorganize the notes. The less organized the lecture, book or journal may be in presentation, the more challenging the opportunity to organize the material. You will discover that well-organized notes will make studying for exams or the composition of papers much easier. But that is not all: the determination to follow this practice during your three years at seminary will pay great dividends for sermon organization throughout your entire ministry.

---

[6]It is excellent practice also to outline sermons as you hear or read them.

SUGGESTED PROJECTS
For Classroom or Study

In the Classroom

1. Prepare an outline and submit it to at least two other students for suggestions and comments. When two other outlines are submitted to you, attach a sheet of paper containing your notations to the original outline before returning it.

In the Classroom or Study

2. Select a printed sermon in which the outline does not clearly appear in the printed form, and outline it for yourself.

3. Prepare a single outline for a persuasive speech (or sermon) but write it out in both an inductive and deductive form.

4. Using the following cards (which you may duplicate on 3 x 5 cards), arrange the body of a speech in good outline form:

Transitions help listeners to recognize the progression of an argument.	There are three things I'd like to suggest as helpful keys to outlining the 3 kinds of speeches.	THREE KEYS TO EFFECTIVE OUTLINING
Use frequent repetition in speeches to motivate.	Bold outlines help listeners understand the divisions of a topic.	Remember, there are 3 keys to the 3 kinds of speeches— Bold outlines (I) Clear transitions (C) Frequent repetitions (M)
Repetition of the major imperative helps to give a sense of urgency.	Transitions help listeners to recognize the implications of facts in an argument.	Use Bold Outlines for speeches to inform.
Use clear transitions for speeches to convince.	Repetition of the major imperative ("Go," "Give") Drives home the main point.	Bold outlines help listeners to remember the divisions of a topic.

In the Study

Arrange to exchange the outlines of your next ten sermons with two or three other ministers for analysis and comments as in suggestion 1 (above).

Chapter Seven

ACQUIRING A PREACHING STYLE

INDIVIDUALITY AND CUSTOM

The word *style* refers to the use of language. Originally the word was connected with *stylus* (or pen) and meant the way a particular individual uses his stylus. Buffon is credited with having said, "Style is the man."[1] This famous statement, along with Christopher Morley's "Style is idiosyncrasy," emphasizes the note of individualism which is inherent in the etymology of the word. Both statements are true as far as they go, but they are partial and unbalanced and, therefore, dangerous. When a speaker thinks of style solely in terms of individual expression, he runs the danger of becoming esoteric. Pushed far enough, such a view of style ultimately leads to the formation of a small clique or cult which alone can appreciate and interpret the style (or in its most extreme form, can be appreciated only by the master himself). This is what has happened whenever the individualism of style has been stressed so strongly in art, music, poetry, or even in theology (cf. Tillich). Good style in communication, therefore, must be balanced with the norms of custom. In maintaining a balance between individual freshness and understandable form, the speaker runs into most of the problems that are connected with style. Good style, then, is individualism within accepted norms. That is to say, while on the one hand one's style may be unique, nevertheless his style must always be *in style* and not out of style. George Campbell says that words, in order to be within the norm, must be: (1) in reputable use; (2) in national use; (3) in present use.[2]

---

[1] *Le Style, c'est L'homme.* Although the source of this statement has been disputed.

[2] George Campbell, *The Philosophy of Rhetoric,* new ed., Harper and

Style fundamentally is language usage, which means the choice and use of words. Good style, therefore, involves the study and practised use of vocabulary, grammar and syntax. The study of style requires some knowledge of semantics (the meaning of words), philology (the history of words) and grammar (the rules and habits of word usage). Style concerns words and how they are put together in the attempt to communicate ideas.

YOU HAVE A STYLE

You must not think of style as something new that you may now begin to acquire. Like the man who was astounded to discover that he had been speaking prose all his life, you must recognize that *you already have a style*. Style cannot be avoided. It is there the minute you open your mouth. It is the manner in which you communicate your thoughts. The real questions with respect to style are questions like these: Is your style vital, alive, interesting, or is it dull, drab and uninviting? Is it clear or muddled? Is it conscious or unconscious? Is it simple or ornate? Is it under control (your servant) or out of control (your master)? Is it flexible and growing or is it rigid, frozen, canned and refrigerated? Is it appropriate or inappropriate to your subject, to your audience and to yourself? Are you cultivating your style daily or has it gone to seed? In short, is your style good or poor?

STYLE AFFECTS CONTENT

Style is important. Wellman, in his historic book, *The Art of Cross-Examination,* rightly says, "There is matter in manner."[3] Richard Weaver wrote:

"Language is not a purely passive instrument... It has a

---

brothers, N. Y.: 1851, pp. 164-168. This seems to describe the original biblical languages perfectly.

[3]Wellman, Francis I., *The Art of Cross-Examination,* Collier Books N. Y.: 1962, p. 35.

set of postures and balances which somehow modify your thrusts and holds . . . You pour into it (the sentence form) your meaning, and it deflects and molds into certain shapes . . . This counter-pressure can be turned to advantage . . . The failure of those who are careless is that they allow the counter-force to impede their design."[4]

It is vital to be aware of the counter-pressure of language. We who believe in the verbal inspiration of the Scriptures know that the choice of the correct word to express a thought is all important. Nothing less conveys the exact meaning. The counter-pressure of language means that wrongly chosen words thrust back at us and reshape our thoughts and mis-shape our communication; sometimes quite seriously. Style, then, tends to add and subtract. That is why the sovereign God who used the different personalities who wrote the Scriptures not only used their distinct styles (which are clear-ly discernible in their writings), but also by his providence pre-pared these writers through their life experiences so that they would develop the styles in which he wanted his Word to be written. The different styles of the biblical writings are them-selves a clear indication of God's concern about this matter. Conservative Christians, of all people, should believe in the cultivation of a clear and effective style. God created Adam and established a relationship with him based upon his Word. The serpent introduced the first langauge problem by ques-tioning that Word. Jesus Christ is called the Word; i.e., God's most effective means of communicating with man, and he has given his special, redemptive revelation in the words of the inspired Scriptures. God has, in every way, dignified language and has shown his great concern for communication by words. That is why every effective preacher of the Word has himself also become a student of words.[5]

---

[4]Weaver, Richard, "Improvement of Writing and Speaking," in the University of Missouri *Bulletin*, Columbia: n. d., p. 8.

[5]Cf. Adams, *Competent to Counsel, op. cit.*, Chapter 10, pp. 211 ff.

THE CASE FOR EXTEMPORANEOUS PREACHING

The case for extemporaneous preaching first may be based upon the fact that in the Scriptures preaching is *always* extemporaneous. Extemporaneous does not mean *unprepared,* but rather speaking in which (after careful preparation) the preacher chooses much of his language at the time of delivery. Extemporaneous speaking does not preclude the use of an outline to which the preacher may make occasional reference. Many of his words may be words that were chosen previously because of their accuracy, precision or crucial importance in making a particular point.

Extemporaneous speaking is preferable also because there is a great difference between oral and written language. Most language training throughout grade school and college years concentrates on writing the English language. This written style is the only style that we have ever been taught to write. Significant studies by Gordon Thomas at Michigan State University showed, however, that an oral style holds at least a ten per cent advantage in comprehension over such a written style.[6] The two styles need to be contrasted because there are essential differences between them. As far back as Aristotle the distinction was noted.[7] Oral English is intended for the ear; written English is intended for the eyes. Oral English proceeds at the speaker's rate, whereas written English moves at the reader's rate. Therefore, more repetition, shorter less complex sentences, and more simple and concrete words are characteristic of good oral English. The listener, unlike the reader, cannot pause and ponder, he cannot reread, he cannot go look up a word in the dictionary. The vocabulary used in effective oral English is smaller, more colorful, less abstract. More of the personality is involved in conveying thought. In addition to language, voice and body may be used in the

---

[6]Buehler and Linkugel, *op. cit.,* pp. 256 ff.

[7]Aristotle, *The Rhetoric,* 3:12.

speaking situation for emphasis and for description. Instant adaptation is possible through immediate response to listener feedback. Omissions, additions, clarifications and alterations may be used in extemporaneous speaking in response to feedback. Thus, more flexibility in meeting audience needs is possible. The oral English form is more conversational. There is free and frequent use of contraction, grammar is less formal, there is more use of the second person, and there is less condensation and telescoping of ideas. It is not as tight as written English. Indeed, editors concerned with written English style also make this point. Russell T. Hitt, editor of *Eternity*, advised against the use of dictating equipment in the writing of magazine articles because "It tends to extreme wordiness."[8]

There is also the possibility in extemporaneous speaking for the use of on-the-spot insights, or for the operation of what I prefer to call the *jelling factor*. Every good extemporaneous preacher, after preaching has written into his outline thoughts that occurred to him while he was preaching that he used on the spot. They just seemed to jell in a way in which they would not jell in the study. Jelling, I must hasten to say, is the *result* of good preparation, and not a replacement for it. The jelling factor is the fruit or culmination of careful preparation and long thought prior to the delivery of the sermon. During the full concentration due to the tension of the preaching experience, at the moment of delivery certain ideas jell. Jelling gives a spontaneity and sparkle to speaking that the calm composition of full manuscripts done solely in the study is unable to bring to it. This is understandable since there is a comparative quiet and lack of tension in the study where full manuscripts are prepared.

It is easier, too, to move from extemporaneous speaking to written than it is to throw away the written crutch. There are

---

[8]In a mimeographed handout, "How to Write Readable Articles," 1958, p. 5. Incidentally, note that Hitt's title contains only three "strong words."

many circumstances in which preachers cannot write out a speech first. A death often occurs during the press of other duties. The preacher must deliver a funeral sermon in two days during which he simply does not have the time to compose a fully prepared manuscript. By the time one has written out his words to speak at a presbytery meeting, it is too late because discussion is over and the motion has already been passed. Moreover, as Sir Walter Raleigh said, "A sea of upturned faces is half the speech."[9] The enthusiasm aroused by the occasion, the worship experience, the audience response, the tension of delivery, etc., are all part of the sermon too. A sermon is not something on paper; it is something delivered by a preacher to his congregation at *that* particular worship service to which *all* of these elements contribute. The inescapable conclusion to which these facts move is that sermons should be tongue-born, not pen-born.

Only an exceptional man is capable of fully writing out and delivering oral English. Schools do not teach how to write oral English; indeed they teach students to write something quite different. It is too late at this point in life (even if it were worth while to do so) and too great a task to teach men in seminary how to write oral English. Yet the only way that full manuscripts can be used profitably is when one learns how to write them in oral English. Few people know how to do it. Hardly anyone has been trained in it, and it is difficult to teach one's self. And even then, when one has learned to write oral English, he still lacks the all-important benefit of the jelling factor. There is usually greater loss of eye contact in reading full manuscripts and there is little or no possibility for adaptation to feedback.[10]

---

[9] Buehler and Linkugel, *op. cit.,* p. 259.

[10] A study of the sermons of Peter Eldersveld and of Joel Nederhood reveals that these men excel in the rare ability of writing oral English. The writer once spoke with Eldersveld's daughter, who said that he spent many hours endeavoring to make his English truly oral. A profit-

FULL FLUENCY IS THE GOAL

The stylistic goal to seek is *full fluency*. Fully fluent speech, like other elements of preaching, calls no attention to itself while it effectively communicates content. Style, like delivery, organization and everything else in the speech, exists for the sake of content. Style is a *means* of bringing the content to the listener, and cannot become an end in itself. Style, therefore, should grow out of and parallel the content just as delivery does. But in order to do so, it must be adapted to and appropriate to the purpose, the speaker, the audience, and the occasion. If it is not so adapted, it will inevitably call attention to itself rather than to God's message.

It is important, therefore, to consider language in relationship to these other factors. But first, consider the following question: "What is full fluency?" Full fluency might be defined as the ability to pick the right words (that is, those which are oral, precise, colorful and psychologically appropriate) at high speed and to put them together in easily understood and dynamic speech.

Full fluency involves proper vocabulary (word) usage. The problem for preachers cannot be solved, as some suppose, by building larger vocabularies. Of course, regular habits of vocabulary building should continue throughout your life. These

---

able study for a student interested in this matter would be to examine Eldersveld's sermons, noting particularly the first words or phrases of paragraphs, the use of contractions and other matters that have to do with oral English. See also the author's review of *Nothing But the Gospel* in the *Westminster Theological Journal*, Vol. XXX, November 1967, No. 1, pp. 125, 126. Nederhood's oral style has improved markedly during the last three years. Remember too that Eldersveld and Nederhood have other problems to overcome that a preacher in a normal congregational speaking situation does not face. They cannot use bodily action over the radio. Neither are they able to depend upon eye contact. There is a certain restriction of volume and emphasis because volume is mechanically controlled on radio. Certain aspects of the voice, such as quality, rate and pitch, must be called into use in new and extended ways for the radio medium, since bodily action must be translated into style and delivery.

principally consist of (1) the regular use of the dictionary to look up the meaning of every word that you do not understand precisely; (2) the proper use and pronunciation of those new words in everyday conversation until they become a part of your speaking vocabulary; and (3) a precise understanding of the connotations as well as the denotation of the word. The basic problem is not that we need larger vocabularies, but, rather, that we need to make larger use of the vocabularies that we already have. The average college student has a large recognition vocabulary of about 250,000 words. Although I know of no reports on the matter, the size of a seminary student's vocabulary can be presumed to far outstrip this number. Yet consider how few of the words he knows that he uses. C. K. Ogden, in speaking of everyday language, says that there are 20,000 common words, of which only 7,000 to 8,000 are in everyday use.[11] Milton used only slightly over 11,000 words and Shakespeare 25,000.[12] The problem, then, is not how large the vocabulary is, but how to use it more flexibly and widely. Some ministers have a habit of buying books to put on their shelves rather than buying books to use. But the value of books is not in how many one accumulates; rather, it lies in the selectivity and use of those books. The same is true of words. As sinful creatures we develop lazy habits that limit our vocabularies. We tend to use stereotype expressions, cliches and trite phrases. John C. Merrill speaks of sermons as "often no more than cliche-ridden discourses easing the listener through another 'duty-period' of religious exposure."[13] We overwork a limited number of words or phrases (the words *look* and *say*, for instance, each

---

[11]In Lester Thonssen and Howard Gilkinson, *Basic Training in Speech*, DC. Heath and Company, Boston: 1953, p. 140.

[12]*Ibid.*, p. 144.

[13]A. Donald Bell and John C. Merrill, *Dimensions of Christian Writing*, Zondervan Publishing House, Grand Rapids: 1970, p. 54

have over 100 cousins with much more pep and accuracy.[14])
By failing to recognize that there is a best word and phrase
for every thought and object, we settle for second rate terms.
One writer says, "Exact words are dynamic; approximate
ones are duds!"[15]

One way to begin to solve the problem of enlarging the use
of one's vocabulary is to start to consciously use more concrete and precise words. Words like *who's it* or *whatch-a-ma-
call-it* are extremes, and yet shading down from these are
dozens of other over-worked abstractions. Be concrete. This
will force you to use more precise terms. Don't speak of a
nice smell, but "the smell of honeysuckle on a sultry summer
evening" (or perhaps, better, a sultry August evening). Abstractions leave too much for the mind and imagination to fill
in. Listeners do not have time to study a word in a speech as
they might in reading written English or as they might study
an abstract painting or poem. The more abstract a painting is,
the more universal it becomes, but the last thing a preacher
wants is a sermon so universal that it has no particularizing
power.

Vocabulary usage is a matter of learned behavior, or habit.
Like every other habit, the proper use of vocabulary must be
developed just about the same way that we develop our muscles. Muscles are not developed by working out once every six
weeks in a tremendous burst of effort. Instead of practicing
for fifteen hours once every other week, a weight lifter would
be wiser to work out briefly *every day* for months. *Regular
practice* is the answer. Practice, using vocabulary to the full
in informal situations every day, is the only key to improvement.

Augustine said, "There is hardly a single eloquent man who

---

[14]Don Wolfe and Elen Geyer, *Enjoying English*, L. W. Singer Company, Inc., Syracuse: 1954, p. 227.

[15]*Ibid.*

can both speak well and think of the rules of eloquence while he is speaking."[16] The formal speaking situation, therefore, in which the speaker must concentrate on *what* he is saying and not *how* he says it, is not the time for practice. Instead he must work on the improvement of vocabulary usage when others are letting down their hair in everyday conversation. Eventually his efforts will pay off as he (and others) will notice that his language has changed in the formal speaking situation as well. This will come in a natural way. Speech *in the pulpit* (whether it is good or poor) is the direct result of speech habits developed *outside* the pulpit.

STYLE AND ITS ADAPTATION

Style must be adapted to the audience, to the occasion, to the speaker and to the purpose. Effective oral style consists of short, simple, colorful sensuous (not sensual)[17] words. Herbert Spencer observed that the words learned in early life have the strongest force and power.[18] If this is true, the suggestion about telling night-time stories mentioned previously becomes doubly important. The kinds of words used in speaking to children are probably the most important kinds of words to use in speaking clearly and forcefully in the pulpit. The early-learned, shorter, more basic words are the best to use; this has been stated as the use of Anglo-Saxon words rather than Latin and Greek derivatives. The former are the most forceful terms in our English language. Yet these must be used (not a few overworked) flexibly and precisely. The 23rd Psalm, for instance, has 118 words, 92 of which in the King James version are of but one syllable. Again, in the first

---

[16]*Christian Instruction*, John J. Garigan, trans., CIMA Publishing company, N. Y.: 1947

[17]Cf. Jay Adams, *Sense Appeal in the Sermons of Charles Haddon Spurgeon*, Masters Thesis, Temple University School of Theology: 1958.

[18]Herbert Spencer, *Philosophy of Style*, Pageant Press, Inc., N. Y.: 1959, pp. 18-20.

118 words of Hamlet's most famous soliloquy, "To be or not to be," 99 of these are of but one syllable. C. E. Jefferson wrote that the preacher's vocabulary

". . . must be made up of words which the people know. The words of the shop and the street and the home are the earthen vessels into which the Heavenly Treasure is to be poured. . . . Every opaque word subtracts from the preacher's power. A preacher's vocabulary ought to be subjected to the refining influence of ordinary conversation. It is in the suds of everyday speech that the starch of the schools must be washed out of the preacher's style. . . . In conversation one is obliged to be sensible. . . . When we converse, our words are simple, and short, our sentences are direct, our style is flexible. . . . A sermon is defective if it sounds bookish."[19]

A preacher's speech, like the *koine* Greek (common everyday Greek) of the New Testament which God chose as the vehicle for his message, ought to be the speech (as Jefferson says) of the home, the street and the shop. This is precisely what *koine* Greek was (cf. I Cor. 2). Tholuck wrote, "Our Lord's mode of address is that of the popular orator; the language he uses is not that of the school."[20] McBurney distinguished between "the language of use" and "the language of art." The former he calls the speaker's "vegetable garden," the latter his "flower garden."[21] It is important to understand that you can't eat flowers. But, it is also appetizing to have a few in the centerpiece while eating. Ralph Waldo Emerson, in his essay, "The Language of the Street," wrote:

[19]Charles E. Jefferson, *The Ministering Shepherd*, New York, Hodder and Stoughton, n.d., p. 162 ff.

[20]A. Tholuck, *Commentary on the Sermon on the Mount*, Smith, English and Company, Philadelphia: 1860, p. 165.

[21]McBurney, *op. cit.*, pp. 25 ff.

"The language of the street is always strong. I confess to some pleasure from the stinging rhetoric of a rattling oath in the mouth of truckmen and teamsters. How brisk it is by the side of a page of the North American Review. Cut these words of the street and they bleed; they are vascular and alive; they walk and run. Moreover, they who use them do not trip in their speech. Their phraseology is a shower of bullets, whilst Cambridge men and Yale men correct themselves and begin again at every half sentence."[22]

Of course, in that quotation you should note the language of Emerson, himself. He speaks of nouns that *bleed,* verbs that *sting* and *rattle.* This is vascular speaking.

Rudolph Flesch, from his studies in comprehension, has concluded that comprehension is aided by: (1) shorter numbers of words in a sentence; (2) shorter numbers of syllables in words; (3) personal rather than abstract terms.[23] Interesting work has been done by the Voice of America broadcasters who invented Special English to teach simple English to foreign audiences and also by C. K. Ogden, who devised Basic English, a limited English language that has only 850 words. In both of these languages the size of the English vocabulary is reduced to a minimum, composed largely of concrete Anglo-Saxon terms. The *Today's English Version* of the New Testament which has become so popular is written largely in Special English. Someone has said that "little minds believe big words signify big ideas."[24] While it would seem important to enlarge one's use of the vocabulary that he already possesses, it would also seem equally important to discover what sort of words ought mostly to be added to one's working vocabulary. Presumably, effort should be made to enrich our vocabularies primarily with *koine-type* terms.

---

[22]In Richard Borden, *op. cit.,* p. 87.

[23]Rudolph Flesch, *The Art of Plain Talk,* Harper and Brothers, N. Y.: 1946, Chapter Seven.

[24]Buhler and Linkugel, *op. cit.,* p. 264.

Spurgeon's effective use of *sensuous* words (words that appeal to the five senses) also is instructive. He early became a master in the use of evocative language, that is, language that vicariously evokes sensory responses.[25] Unlike most preachers, Spurgeon appealed to all five senses, though not as much to the sense of taste as to the other four (he lived on a restricted diet). Most men learn how to appeal to only one sense, if indeed they learn sensuous appeal at all, namely, the sense of sight. Most discussion has, therefore, centered around acquiring the ability to paint word pictures.

One can paint pictures by describing size, shape and color, but he can appeal also to the sense of touch by describing a texture as rough, smooth, hot, cold, hard, soft, etc.; a taste as sweet, sour, salty, bland; an odor as fragrant or foul; and a sound as loud, soft, harsh, pleasant, distinct, muffled. He may speak evocatively of mountains of potatoes, lakes of gravy, fields of peas, forests of roast beef, and for dessert a Niagara of whipped cream cascading over cliffs of apricots and peaches.

In acquiring good style the trick is to learn how to trim off the fat while keeping the meat well marbled. This is one of the preacher's most difficult tasks. The extremes here are both temptations, but usually the greater temptation is to serve too much fat. Sermons must be prepared carefully, well garnished, served hot by candlelight, and sometimes with flowers on the table. Sermons must not be tossed out in chunks as slabs of raw meat are served to tigers in the zoo. The most tasty meat is well marbled meat; this gives it flavor. While economizing on words as, for instance, by avoiding circumlocutions, the preacher cannot feed his congregation meat that is too lean. And even the choicest roast or steak is unpalatable for human consumption when raw.

Beza once said of Calvin's sermons, "Every word weighs a

---

[25]Cf. Jay Adams, *Sense Appeal In the Sermons of Charles Haddon Spurgeon, op. cit.*

pound."[26] And yet, we must remember in reading the work of Calvin that the style is largely oral, not written. Calvin dictated in bed. Although there is no unnecessary fat, his preaching is not bookish; sentences, for instance, are not too compressed. Vocabulary is exact, but not pedantic. Richard Borden speaks of "Word Wax."[27] Borden recalls that the Roman sculpturers sometimes concealed surface cracks in their marble statues with melted beeswax that was of a similar color. A few weeks later, when the wax dried out and crumbled away, it left the cracks exposed. Therefore, speaking should be *sincere* (that word means "without wax"). Borden urges speakers to carve speeches out of words and to use no wax. Various sorts of wax need to be removed:

(1) *Superlatives.* Speech often can be strengthened by removing superlatives. Superlatives qualify and thus limit. If they are used too frequently or if they are used indiscriminately there is no way to emphasize material that is significant enough to require the superlative.

(2) *Trite, stale expressions.*

(3) *Meaningless repetitions.* Here it is crucial to stress the word *meaningless.*

(4) *Additives* like "and so forth" which contribute nothing.

(5) *Weasel words.* These are unnecessary qualifying words that fail to commit one when he ought to be committed.

(6) *Run-on sentences.* Borden says about the latter, "To be grammatically sure-footed use plenty of periods."[28] Learn to freckle your speech with periods.

Transitional materials are not fat; they constitute the nec-

---

[26]*Tot verba Tot pondera.* A. W. Blackwood, *Preaching From the Bible.* Abingdon-Cokesbury Press, 1941, pp. 75 ff.

[27]Richard Borden, *Public Speaking As Listeners Like It,* Harper, N. Y.: 1935.

[28]*Ibid.,* p. 80.

124

essary muscles, tendons and ligaments that hold the several parts of the body of the message together. Borden says:

"Use good connective tissues . . . don't treat sentences like strung sausages. Button some together. Try a hook and eye with others. Experiment with the zipper fastening. Develop skill with a square knot and the half hitch."

The English language is rich in connectives. Therefore, there is no need for sameness. There can be a tremendous amount of variety. Yet speakers tend to settle for a narrow band of this transitional spectrum.[29]

ADAPTING STYLE TO AUDIENCE AND OCCASION

Good speakers speak on a variety of language levels and have flexibility of style. You do not wear the same clothes on every occasion; when going fishing, going to church, or before painting the front porch, you dress appropriately. Language is the dress of your thought. At the home, at the office, at school, before a group of scientists, speaking to a third-grade Sunday School class, at a banquet, at a funeral, you should speak differently. You must learn to speak in a way that is adapted to and appropriate to each of these occasions and audiences. That is to say, your language level is determined not only by the topic, but also by the audience and the occasion.

Paul wrote, "Except you utter words easy to be understood, how shall it be known what is spoken? For you speak into the air" (I Cor. 14:9). Often a preacher is guilty of this offense. One way in which he offends is by becoming overly formal in speech. His words are wearing a dress suit while he is attending a fish fry. For example, it is foolish for a minister to make an announcement about the Boys Brigade using the

---

[29]In preaching informative sermons, there is, for example, a tendency to introduce new units of thought with an overuse of the word "now."

same vocabulary, solemnity and force that he would use in preaching the doctrine of election. Audiences differ, of course, according to age, knowledge, attitudes, and in many other ways. What is fitting on one occasion also is ineffective, absurd, or even insulting on another. Wisdom and judgment in the use of words and language level, therefore, are essential. It is helpful to ask yourself, "What will be the general mood of the meeting? Will it be formal or informal, jovial or solemn, light or serious?"

The base from which to operate, however, is the *koine* mentioned previously, that is, the business language of modern society plus a heightening to which the subject matter of the Scriptures naturally elevates it. We move up and down from that language level according to whether we are speaking at the local ministerium or to a group of teen agers at a hot dog roast.

Technical terms are of importance. May Chrsitian technical terms be used in this day in which there is such an illiteracy with respect to Christian language as well as content? On the one hand, there is need to re-educate people biblically, which means that they must be taught again the great scriptural terms. But on the other hand, there are circumstances when it is better to avoid the use of these terms temporarily. First, Christian technical terms should be avoided when people are not ready to hear them; that is, when they won't understand them or they are offensive because of misunderstanding, and will repel listeners. Secondly, they might also be avoided when the people are too ready to hear them; that is, when these terms have become so familiar to the listener that they no longer have impact, but instead have become warm, familiar, old friends used as jargon without meaning. A preacher once read a passage from a modern translation in which Paul condemned homosexuality. At the door following the sermon a woman chided the speaker for using "vulgarity in the pulpit." For years she had read the passage "abusers of themselves with mankind" without the slightest understanding. The new translation had for the first time brought home the exact import of Paul's words. Unfortunately, she didn't see it that way.

THE FORCE AND POWER OF WORDS

Force and power lie not only in ideas, but also in the words by which they are conveyed. Therefore, it is essential to avoid the use of weak, as well as inaccurate, words. While strictly speaking words may be accurate, at the same time they may be weak. One reason for weakness lies in the overuse of passive constructions. Active verbs are stronger than passive verbs. Active verbs pack a punch. Reread the last sentence in the passive: a punch is packed by active verbs. Take another example or two: "I think" is more forceful than "It is my thought," or "See your dentist" is more potent than "Your dentist is to be consulted." The passive has its place, but frequently preachers overwork it and, thereby, destroy its legitimate use.

FIGURES OF SPEECH

There are many figures of speech, but we will mention only a few.

Simile and *Metaphor.* A simile is a phrase introduced by the words *like* or *as:* "The kingdom of heaven is like . . ." A parable is in effect an extended simile. A metaphor is the use of a phrase like the one Jesus used when he called Herod "that fox." An allegory is fundamentally an extended metaphor. Avoid mixed metaphors; don't have "someone biting the hand that lays the golden egg." The Bible is full of simile and metaphor; there is no better place to study this figure than in the Scriptures themselves.

Personification and *Apostrophe.* Death is personified in I Corinthians 15:55-58 (quoting Hosea 13:14) and then addressed in an apostrophe (speaking to the personification): "O death where is thy victory; O death where is thy sting?"

Personification is used boldly in Proverbs 8 where wisdom is personified as a good woman who is going about the street using all the wiles of the harlot to woo the young man to herself rather than to the harlot.

Parallelism. Parallelism is a device used largely in Hebrew poetry where the *repetition* of the main idea is the genius of the poetical form and this repetition usually occurs in parallel lines. The meanings of the first and the second lines are identical in synonymous poetry. In antithetical poetry, the meaning of the second line contrasts with the first. This poetical form is used throughout the Psalms, Book of Proverbs, and elsewhere in the Scriptures. It also gets into the thinking, writing and speaking of the New Testament preachers. There is a different type of parallelism in I Corinthians 13, where phrases are repeated in parallel form. The repetition of the form "Though I . . . and have not charity" (I Cor. 13) is typical of this sort of parallelism.

Antithesis. II Corinthians 4:5 provides a good example of antithesis: "What we preach is not ourselves, but Jesus Christ as Lord." See also I Corinthians 2:4.

Onomatopoeia. These are sound effect or sound-like-it words. Buzz, bang, boom, slam, meow, moo are all sound-effect words. Preaching in Baltimore, Donald Gray Barnhouse once declared that the view usually denominated as post tribulation premillennialism "is SSSSSatanic!" As he said it, you could hear the serpent hiss. This was a more subtle form of *Onomatopoeia.*

Rhetorical Questions. Expected replies are implied in the question. Job has a chapter full of them (cf. Chapter 38). The rhetorical nature of these questions is typically misunderstood and misapplied by Mormons who take the question, "Where were you when I created . . ." literally as though God were speaking of pre-existence. Job 38 is also a fine example of the question cluster, a rhetorical form used in all great preaching. Question clusters consist of a series of questions, one following another, usually paralleling one another in form and rising to a climax. Question clusters normally occur in emotionally heavy portions of a sermon.

The Periodic Sentence. This is a sentence with suspense, where the main thought and climax of the sentence comes at the end (cf. Matt. 25:31, R.S.V., and I Cor. 15:54). A periodic sentence begins with a predicate, putting the conditional element first, and then ends with the subject. This is the reverse of the normal sentence order in English.

The study of style, then, is of great importance to the preacher. For the rest of his life he will cultivate a better style. He will use every means available to improve. He will turn to his wife's cookbooks to learn how to give clear, simple, understandable how-to directions. He will study newspaper accounts to discover the secrets of colorful reporting. He will listen to children talking to one another and will avidly read their storybooks with a view to upgrading his narrative techniques. And what he learns he will use regularly. Words are the tools of thought. They should be kept clean, well-oiled and sharp by constant use and attention. Good tools, used skillfully, help us build the case we wish to make. Let us become expert craftsmen of the Word. In summary, the whole realm of language usage will become his textbook so that he may develop the most flexible, varied, useful and appropriate style that he can in order to proclaim the whole counsel of God more effectively in every situation.

SUGGESTED PROJECTS
For Classroom or Study

In the Classroom or Study

1. Dictate (using a tape recorder) a paragraph of original illustrative material attempting to apply the principles of good style learned in this chapter. Play back and copy down the paragraph in writing. Notice the oral style. Trying not to destroy the oral nature of the paragraph, improve the style. Then read the new paragraph onto a tape and listen to the improvement. Preserve the original and compare the two. Both tapes and the written transcripts may be brought to class for review.
2. Analyze your own oral style and determine its strengths and weaknesses. Perhaps you will want to use a tape recording to help you.
3. Make a growing list of biblical similes and metaphors.

In the Classroom

1. Write a two-page report to be delivered to the class on some one element of style you have discovered in the sermons recorded in the Book of Acts.
2. Discuss the use of "slang" as it does or does not relate to a *koine* style.

Chapter Eight

DELIVERING THE GOODS
(With the Voice)

A PHILOSOPHY OF DELIVERY

A preacher must not only have the goods, but also must know how to deliver the goods. *Delivery* concerns all of those visible and audible aspects of speaking that we usually group under the words voice and body. This is the aspect of speech that makes it unique and distinct from other forms of communication and, as a result, is of the greatest importance to preachers. It is delivery that gives the preacher an advantage over the written page. But along with all of its advantages, delivery also involves the speaker in complex, wide-ranging, multi-disciplined studies relating to such diverse areas as psychology, physiology, physics, medicine, anatomy, neurology, dentistry, biology, and phonetics. Yet the philosophy is simple enough: delivery must grow out of and complement content at every point. This has been discussed already in the chapter on narrative speaking. At all points in the reliving of the experience, delivery becomes natural when the speaker feels what he says. The particular use of voice and body required at any given point in the message is determined by the content as an aid to making it known.

THE MECHANICS OF VOICE PRODUCTION

Voice means more than *sound.* What is the difference between sound and voice, and what is the relationship between the two? *Sound* is unarticulated air in vibration, whereas *voice* is articulated air in vibration. Unarticulated air is air that has not been shaped by the vocal apparatuses into speech; articulated air has been. The physics of sound is a quite complex study and not really essential to a practical understanding of what to do in speaking. One of the best complete but simplified explanations of the physics of sound has been published

130

by the Bell Telephone Company. For more information consult this volume.[1]

However, there are certain facts that need to be discussed at some length with respect to the mechanics of speech. Speech production may be divided into four phases. The first phase is *breathing*. There is much misinformation concerning breathing. Breathing is not a problem at all for most speakers. Shoulder raising habits and exercises in so-called diaphragmatic breathing are useless in improving one's breathing for speech. In the first place, all breathing is diaphragmatic. Without the use of the diaphragm you could not breathe at all. Most breathing exercises are a waste of time for speakers. The most common "breathing" problem is running out of breath at the end of a sentence so that it fades out at the end. But this supposed "breathing" problem is more likely a problem of style. The solution probably does not lie in breathing exercises, but rather in adopting a new style in which shorter, less complex sentences (than the one that I am now involved in) are used.

How does one breathe? Note the following diagram.

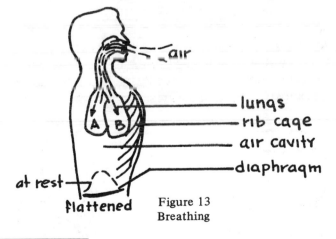

Figure 13
Breathing

[1]Peter Denes and Elliot N. Pinson, *The Speech Chain*, Waverly Press, Inc., Baltimore: 1963.

The lungs (A and B) suck in the air. This happens when there is less pressure on the lungs from the air surrounding them that is caught inside the body cavity than there is on the air outside the body. Thus, the greater pressure outside the body drives the air down into the lungs. How is air pressure reduced inside the body? The pressure of the captured air inside the body surrounding the lungs is reduced whenever the area in which it exists is enlarged in size. This enlargement takes place when by muscular action the dome-shaped diaphragm at the base of the air cavity flattens, enlarging the capacity of the chest cavity containing the air.

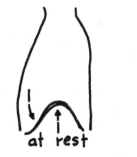
at rest

air cavity area increased
flattened

Figure 14
The Diaphragm

At the same time, usually, there is a further enlargement of the chest area due to the rib cage rising and thereby enlarging the area horizontally as well as vertically. The rib cage at rest is like a bucket with its handle at rest.

Figure 15
Bucket Handle at Rest

As the handle is raised, it not only rises vertically, but also moves horizontally out away from the bucket.

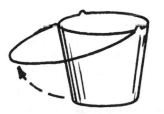 

Figure 16
Bucket Handle Raised

When the diaphragm relaxes to its normal position in which it is humped like a dome and the rib cage drops down and in, the air in the chest cavity is compressed, presses against the lung and squeezes the air out through the nose and mouth.

Phonation. The second phase in speech is phonation, which produces the activated stuff out of which speech is carved.

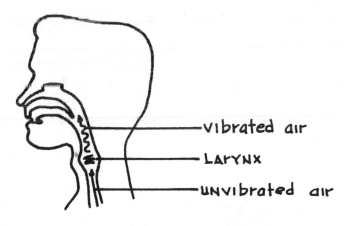

Figure 17
The Larynx

A vibration is set up by the air that is forced out of the lungs when it strikes the vocal folds. Here four factors may be distinguished. These are volume, pitch, rate, and quality. *Volume* is the amplitude or force of the compression against the folds. This determines the loudness of the voice as perceived by the listener. *Pitch* will be higher or lower according to the tension in the folds. Here a fundamental tone is set up. *Rate* has to do with the number of words that can be spoken per second. Rate involves a combination of both phonation and articulation. *Quality* begins with phonation but also has to do with the texture of the mouth. It is affected by the overtones and the fundamental tones as they resonate. Quality describes the variety of textures of sound that are designated by such adjectives as growling, gravelly, soothing, mellow, whining or strident.

Resonance is the third phase of voice production. Resonance is too complex to discuss in detail. Consult Denes and Pinson for more information.[2] Fundamentally, resonance involves sympathetic vibrations which are set up in the chambers of the larynx, the throat, the mouth and the nose. These vibrations tend to swell and/or dampen the tones of the sound. These chambers may be changed in size, shape, and texture by opening and closing the mouth, by the tension that is placed upon the organs, etc. The effects of change in size and shape can be demonstrated simply by changing the shape of the mouth as one continues to speak the word oooh or as he strikes his cheek with a finger while making the change.

Articulation (which includes pronunciation) is the final phase of voice production. Articulation is the shaping of sounds into words. Clear and exact utterances of the sounds in one's language is essential to proper understanding and communication. Articulation is the moulding of resonated sound into identifiable words according to the accepted standards of a language. Functionally, articulation takes place

---

[2]*Op. cit.*

through the modification of phonated (vibrated) air by stopping, hindering, or shaping it. The articulators are the mouth, the tongue, the teeth and the lips. Articulation is learned. Since they are due to faulty learning, articulatory difficulties are also the simplest to correct. Fortunately, most speech problems fall into this category. Articulation may be the cause of what at first seems to be an entirely different sort of speech problem. Initial attention to articulation frequently means reaching a solution to various other difficulties. For instance, a problem may be diagnosed as inability to hear due to lack of volume. Yet this sort of problem often is not a matter of volume at all, but rather a matter of sloppy articulation. When a speaker cannot be understood at a distance, the first thing to do is to try to sharpen his articulation to see if this clears up the problem. When he dots his verbal i's and crosses his verbal t's at the same volume, the chances are that he now may be able to be heard and understood all the way to the back of the room. Articulation should be checked first when one suspects a volume problem, because increasing volume unnecessarily also may increase the wear and tear upon the vocal folds, and this can lead to serious consequences. So, articulation should be checked first, then rate, and then—and only then—volume.

Pronunciation is the sum of most, if not all, of the audible characteristics in a word. Standard and substandard speech is determined by the usage of the better speakers in each of the three acknowledged speech areas of the United States. the Eastern American Speech Area (New England), the Southern American Speech Area (Dixie), and the General American Speech Area (the rest of the country). Of course, there are sub areas within each of these. For example, the mountain dialect, the Middle Atlantic States, where the three speech areas overlap, the large metropolitan areas, the ethnic clusters within them, and the Negro dialect, all form subdivisions, some according to area and others according to groups. *A Pronouncing Dictionary of American English* is the standard reference to the proper pronunciation of American English.[3] In this work Kenyon and Knott distinguish the standard pronunciations for each speech area.

A question for young preachers to ponder is whether or not to change regional patterns of speech. The first part of the answer to that question is that they must be changed if the regional speech contains many substandardisms. Every preacher should endeavor to speak the standard speech of one of the three speech regions. But what about changing to General American speech rather than continuing to use Eastern American or Southern American speech? Many preachers move around the country, although some stay within a restricted speech area. Mass Media, moving populations, and many other forces are rapidly leveling American speech. A young preacher probably ought to work toward the sort of General American speech that has become the standard for television and radio. Dean Rusk was quizzed by a reporter from the University of Missouri Speech Department about this question after he had given a speech in the area. He said that early in his career he had concluded that he must erase most of his former Georgia accent in order to become more acceptable and useful to a larger number of people. Preachers for various reasons may answer the problem differently; but at least they should come to grips with it.

HELP FOR A DOZEN COMMON VOICE DISORDERS

Breathiness. We all are familiar with the sound that has been designated by various terms but here is called *breathiness.* It is the sound of words spoken to the accompaniment of large amounts of unarticulated air. Women sometimes affect this sound because it is thought to sound sexy. The cause of the phenomenon is that the speaker's vocal folds are not closing tightly enough against one another. Breathiness, rather

---

[3]John Kenyon and Thomas Knott, *A Pronouncing Dictionary of American English,* G. C. Merriam Company, Publishers, Springfield: 1953.

than indicating sexual prowess, frequently occurs in people who are less alert, who exert too little tension in speaking, and who are less animated. That is, they are often persons who are too relaxed, usually because they are lazy or simply do not care. Breathiness is, in effect, breath wastage. Unvibrated air escapes as it does when whispering. A portion of the air is not being used in order to articulate and speak words. People with this problem notice that they tend to run out of breath too soon and are often unable to speak an entire sentence without having to snatch a breath in the middle of the sentence. Such people also tend to have choppy phrasing in their speech. They frequently chew and swallow the final words of a sentence or allow the sentence to trail off at the end before it is completed. Usually this problem is due to habit, though it also may develop from nodes (explained later in this chapter) or inflammation of the folds. The first step, then, is to have a physical examination by a physician to be sure that there is no physiological difficulty (such as nodes). Having ascertained this, the solution to the problem lies in learning how to tense the folds to approximate one another through speech training. Of course, personality change may be required in some instances.

Hoarseness. Hoarseness is closely related to breathiness. The condition may be due to a cold or throat inflammation causing the edges of the folds to become so irritated and swollen that the swellings on one or both of the folds keep the folds from closely approximating. Thus, unvibrated air is expelled. Hoarseness usually is the result of any serious inflammation of the larynx. Inflammation of the larynx produces changes in the mucosa of the larynx, and the mucosal change affects the true cords. They are roughened or thickened and the patient becomes hoarse. The real solution to this problem is rest for the voice. This may be achieved by not speaking until the condition clears up. In addition to rest, several other courses of action are open. Sometimes an astringent, such as chili pepper in water, is useful as a gargle. Eucalyptus and menthol drops now packaged and sold by various firms are also helpful. Astringents help reduce the inflammation. The use of a cold steam vaporizer while sleeping allows the process of osmosis to take place, removing some of the fluids in the inflamed areas by that process, and thus reducing the inflammation. Sometimes at the outset of hoarseness, raising or lowering the pitch level of speech will help.[4] Trying to speak below or above one's optimum pitch may cause hoarseness. If hoarseness persists, of course, you should see a physician. There are more than fifty separate known causes of hoarseness. So, it is sometimes very difficult to determine precisely what the source of the problem may be.

Sore Throat, Laryngitis. Hoarseness, sore throat and laryngitis are all interrelated. Any of these conditions may be caused by infections or abuse. Yelling at a football game (or in a sermon) causes such a pounding of the folds against one another when tense that they soon may become sore. Smoking can cause laryngitis. But whatever the cause, the cure is rest and relaxation. Sleeping with a cold steam vaporizer may help. The teapot-cone method, which has some dangers attached to it (such as scalding your throat), may bring quick relief. First you put the teapot on the stove, and then as the steam pours out, you fold up a cone of paper, capturing the steam in the larger opening. Then point the cone down the throat toward the inflamed area. But if you burn yourself, don't blame me: I warned you!

The chief symptom of laryngitis is hoarseness. Sometimes when an infection is present, throat lozenges containing a topical anesthetic will afford relief from pain. But the presence of infection should indicate the need for seeing your physician. DeWeese and Sanders, in their textbook on *Otolaryngology,* say that a saline solution is "as effective as any drugs advocated." They claim that the throat, when hoarse and

---

[4]Depending upon which one is extreme.

sore and on the verge of laryngitis, ought to be cleansed with a warm saline solution. The dose they suggest is one level teaspoonful of salt in one pint of water, or one-half teaspoonful in an ordinary drinking glass. They also suggest that irrigation (which is running the water down through the throat) is better than gargling, though the latter is useful.[5] Aerosol therapy sprays may be used in the room. These help in congestion as well as relieving sore throats. Chewing fennel (or fennelgreek) seeds is an excellent early remedy. Obviously all of these suggestions are nothing more than that; consult a physician early if there is no immediate relief.

Vocal Nodes. Vocal nodes are callouses that develop on one or the other side (or on both sides) of the folds. These contact ulcers, as they are sometimes called, develop from the misuse of the folds over a period of time, especially when the voice is used to speak during a seige of laryngitis. The pounding of tense or sore folds at such a time further aggravates the problem, and nodes may result. It is usually not wise or heroic to preach when your folds are sore. You may cause nodes to develop that, as a result, will keep you quiet for months afterward. Hoarseness is the first sign of nodes and eventual loss of the voice is the second. The treatment, unfortunately (and I should make this very clear) is first, silence, absolute silence! Perhaps you will be required to remain silent for as long as a month or two to see if that will cure the condition. If that does not work, the nodes will have to be removed surgically. Surgery may be followed by another period of two or three months' silence. Finally, after all of this, it may be necessary to take special voice lessons to learn how to avoid doing further damage to the folds. This whole process can extend over a period of months, during which preaching will be totally curtailed. So the heroics of preaching with a sore throat turns out in the long run to be nothing but

---

[5]DeWeese and Sanders, *Textbook on Otolaryngology,* St. Louis: 1960, C. V. Mosby Company, p. 77.

foolhardiness. It is wise for a preacher not to preach (and particularly not to yell) when his voice is sore and hoarse. It is better to get rest for the voice and to call in someone else to preach at that time.

Post-Nasal Drip. Unchecked post-nasal drip irritates the throat, and can lead to the previously considered conditions. Here many suggestions can be made, but the problem for the preacher to solve is to find fast-acting medication that has no side effects and that stops the drip for at least two hours during the morning service. The physician can give you helpful pills. You should tell him, however, that you want medicine that will not make you drowsy. You may be able to use certain patent medicine cures available without a prescription to stop the drip, but most of these have unwanted side effects because they contain antihistamines. Such medication is in abundance at the counter of the drugstore. But while antihistamines may arrest the post-nasal drip, they also may tend to dull one's thinking. So avoid any product that warns, "may cause drowsiness" or, "do not drive or use machinery," since those side effects are also detrimental to speaking. What a preacher needs, therefore, is the kind of oral medicines or local application with no side effects that will give him at least an hour or two of relief while he is preaching. Certain nebulizers on the market fit this description. A nebulizer is a plastic tube which can be squeezed as one inhales. Medication squirts from the tip of it directly onto the area that is congested. One must be careful, however, in the use of these, and ought to confer with his doctor about their use.

Nasality, Densaslity. Nasality may be defined as that foghorn quality in which a speaker nasalizes other letters in addition to *m, n* or *ng*. In English it is proper to nasalize only those three sounds. Of course to speak French, you must learn to nasalize other sounds as well. Americans have learned to nasalize certain sounds and to denasalize others, just as the French have learned to nasalize and denasalize a different set of sounds. Therefore, the answer to this problem is learning; it is a matter of drill in proper speech habits.

Denasality occurs when a speaker does not nasalize the *m*, the *n*, or the *ng* sounds. Denasality sometimes is confused by amateurs with nasality. But denasality can easily be identified by pinching your nose and speaking words that contain an *m*, *n*, or *ng* (e.g., "I have something clogging my nose). It is the sound that you hear when there are obstructions in the nose, due to colds or enlarged adenoids (which may require an operation, if severe). Or denasality may also be a matter of habit. Whenever learned, denasality requires better control of the soft pallet. Drill, again, is the answer to the problem. Nasality and denasality also may stem from psychological causes. Some persons have learned to react to stress by developing nasal systems, for example. Emotional responses to problems of various sorts may affect the way that one's nose operates. Particularly, it may have something to do with giving rise to stuffiness or dryness of the nose or, on the other hand, increased nasal discharge. The answer to this is not medication but change in the patterns of handling life's problems.

Harshness, Stridency, Tinniness. This condition variously described by the three words that head this paragraph (or others) is usually caused by undue tension in the folds. When the folds are brought together too tight, or when they are stretched too tight, harshness, stridency and tinniness is the effect. This is an effect resulting from the texture of the walls of the vocal passages, and particularly from the texture of the vocal folds themselves. If the folds are stretched too tight, they become hard in texture, and as the sound hammers against a hard substance it produces a tinny effect. Usually the pitch is also too high and this is an accompanying sign of the undue tenseness that exists. The answer usually is learning to relax. Relaxing in general will bring relaxation of the vocal musculature. Often it is important to drill on yawning and sighing prior to speaking. When one yawns his muscles naturally relax. Preachers with tinny voices must learn how to yawn so that their audiences won't.

Pitch Problems. Speaking at too high or too low a pitch is usually a matter of habit. When the pitch is too high it is because the folds are overly tense. High pitch also may have a psychological base in anxiety. Or it is possible that the high pitch is a vestige of childhood. When the voice changes took place, the speaker simply continued to speak as if no change had occurred. Even though his folds became longer and thicker than they were before, providing him with the equipment to speak in a deeper, more mature masculine voice, he has never learned how to do it. The solution in such cases of habit is to learn how to speak at optimum pitch. The optimum pitch is the healthiest, easiest, clearest, ringing note for speech. It is the speaker's normal, easiest, most natural speaking pitch. Each individual has his own optimum pitch level. The optimum pitch is the note on the scale that should be the base from which one operates. It is the note from which he moves upward when he is tense and downward when he is more relaxed. Every person has an optimum pitch, but the optimum pitch of one individual may not be the same as that of another. Here are four methods for finding optimum pitch. You may use any or all of them. It is better to use more than one as a check.

First, you may sing up and down the scale and find the upper and lower limit to which you can sing without strain. Next, using a piano, locate the middle note between these two extremes. The tone you are looking for ought then to be located about one-third below this mid-point. That note would be your optimum pitch.

Another way of finding optimum pitch would be to relax in a chair, with your arms hanging down loosely, your legs as loose as possible, your head and neck relaxed and hanging loose. Then, sigh in a vocalized fashion. Do it again and again. Listen for the pitch level. Find that level on the piano, and it should be close to your optimum pitch.

A third means of finding optimum pitch uses reading material. Read as normally as you can. Listen for a central pitch tendency from which you move up and down. Sustain a vowel; note the pitch. Compare it with the vocalized sigh and the tone one-third below the mid-point in singing.

Lastly, you may sing down the scale to the lowest note you can sing comfortably. Then on the piano go up five semitones (that is, five piano keys), and this ought to be on or close to your optimum pitch. The optimum pitch for most men is at about C below middle C.

Articulatory Problems. The largest group of speech problems falls into this category, and fortunately these are the most easily solved. They are all habitual, learned problems. Ear training (learning to hear the error when you speak) followed by retraining through drill, constitute the means by which one may change any articulatory liabilities into articulatory assets. Into this area fall lisping, lip laziness, sloppy articulation and other bad speech habits. Over-articulation, that is articulation which is so precise that it calls attention to itself, is also a serious problem.[6] All articulatory problems have easy and simple solutions for those who are properly motivated to solve them.

Ministerial Whines, Drones, Tunes. There are habits that some preachers have picked up or developed on their own that have been called by a variety of terms. They usually involve a combination of pitch-rate melody patterns. These are those intolerable sounds made by preachers that seem to be peculiar to the profession. The ministerial whine, tune or drone at some time in church history was developed by certain preachers who doubtless felt that it added a note of sanctity or authority to what they had to say. As a matter of fact,

---

[6]E.g., some preachers get into the habit of pedantically pronouncing the words *a* and *the, eh* and *thee* whenever they occur, rather than using the normal pronunciations *uh* and *thuh* whenever possible.

these whines actually turn people off. Nothing is more detestable and disgusting than to hear preachers whining from the pulpit. The message of God is the virile Gospel of the God who as Father sent his Son to the cross for his people. And the Son had the manly determination to go. Jesus Christ came from a carpenter's shop. He was not a Casper Milquetoast or a sissified pantywaist. He was a man. These tunes emasculate the man of God of all of his manly qualities. Years ago C. E. Jefferson wrote, "If certain creatures could hear their pulpit tones, they would be exceedingly amused." Today, with the widespread use of tape recorders, every preacher can enter into this source of amusement, and if he suspects that this problem is his, I advise him to do so.[7]

Such patterns may be broken up (1) by becoming conscious of them, (2) by understanding how seriously they detract and misrepresent the Christian message by calling attention to themselves, and (3) by learning how to preach in a more natural and manly speaking voice. Tunes and whines lack pitch-rate variety. The same kinds of melody patterns occur again and again. So in order to "bust" the pattern, a preacher must learn how to vary rate and pitch. This may be accomplished most rapidly by daily practice in learning to "relive" stories while speaking. He must learn how to let content influence form rather than to shape content by form.

Monotones. A monotone may involve a hearing loss, so the first step is to have one's hearing tested professionally. Not only may a physician do this, but all university speech departments of any size have testing equipment. A monotone involves pitch and/or rate inflexibility. Monotony is the technique used in hypnosis. Nothing then could be more devastating to preaching. The monotone, if it does not result from a hearing loss, is learned behavior. Usually the habit is connected with personality. When this is true, one must also learn

---

[7]Charles E. Jefferson, *op. cit.*, p. 163.

how to become a different person. He must learn how to throw himself, including his emotions, into his speaking. He must learn the proper use of reliving his experience in speaking; he must learn to become more outgoing. In short, he must learn to expose his feelings outwardly to others. Usually the problem with such people is that they will not allow others to know what they are thinking and feeling. A preacher must be willing to allow the Word of God to grasp him inwardly and preach it to others with the same effectiveness and power that it has had upon him.

One's voice tells a lot about a person. Charles Berry, the astronauts' physician, says that he can tell a great deal from just hearing the communications from the astronauts as they are traveling in space. The sound of their voice tells him, for example, whether they are excited or whether they have undue fatigue. The voice is also a clue to one's personality. People with monotones, like those with over-anxiety, sometimes need counseling. The goal for a speaker with a monotone problem is voice variety. He should seek to develop a voice that sparkles with change.

Verbal Pause. A verbal pause is the use of "uh, and uh, er" and other such fillers. There are several theories as to why the verbal pause occurs. One theory is that in modern competitive society if you don't hang on to it, you soon lose the leadership in conversation, and that the use of verbal pauses is one way to hold on. Well, whether this is so or not really matters little. There is a solution to this problem, the same one offered for all other poor speech patterns that involve substituting a new habit for an old one. By conscious practice in normal life circumstances one can soon develop the capacity to eliminate most *uhs* and other verbal pauses. Concurrently, he ought to work on pauses that punctuate. He must become aware of the true purpose of non-verbal pause. He must learn how to use dead air effectively. There is power in pause. Pause enables an audience to allow the previous thought to sink in. It underlines or sets off material and gives time for reflection. It allows one to build suspense and anticipation, and "sets up" the audience for a climax.

Speakers also should learn to avoid pauses after prepositions and articles (these are unnatural spots). Perhaps the most important advice of all is to agree to forfeit 50 cents toward a new hat for your wife every time you use a verbal pause *and have her keep score.* You will soon be broke, but cured.

SUGGESTED PROJECTS
For Classroom or Study

In the Classroom or Study

1. Whether or not you think you have difficulty with pitch, use one or more of the methods suggested and discover your optimum pitch. Check this against tape recordings of your voice (expecially those previously recorded).

   My optimum pitch is _____

2. If you discover that the description of any one or more of the dozen voice disorders mentioned fits you, determine what you will do about it. Ask: should I see a physician, should I speak to my speech instructor, or can I work up a personal improvement program for myself? If a problem is apparent, make plans to do something about it *now*. Your voice is too valuable an asset to the Church of Christ for you to neglect it.

3. Whether you have a voice disorder or not, determine 3-5 areas in which you think you need to improve your speaking ability, and in a two-page paper draw up a *personal improvement program* for yourself that can be carried on over the next three years. If you are taking classroom work, hand in the carbon copy (you should retain a copy as a reminder) to your instructor so that he may be able to check you out from time to time. The paper should contain:

   1. *My problems* as I now see them. State each clearly and succinctly.

   2. *My goals* during the next three years. Goals should include both solutions to problems and anticipated improvements.

   3. *The means* I intend to use to reach these goals.

Chapter Nine

DELIVERING THE GOODS
(With the Body)

Delivery involves not only the use of voice, but also bodily action, which also has been called body speech, body language, visible speech, and the sign language of speech. The philosophy for bodily delivery is precisely the same as that which has been set forth for verbal delivery: delivery should grow out of and supplement content. Bodily delivery is often ludicrous when it does not. We all are familiar with the preacher who wears a Liberace smile that does not fit the content of what he says. The body at every point should aid the content rather than call attention to itself. Few women were ever won by men who shook their fists in their faces and shouted, "I love you." Yet preachers try to preach grace and God's love that way. Then there is the preacher who is always very proper and solemn and unemotional, even when speaking of God's love and Christian joy. This kind of man by the rest of his body distorts the truth of God's Word that is upon his lips. Delivery in its bodily form can make all the difference in speech. By delivery, a preacher can completely deny everything that he says. Is that going too far? Well, what if he simply gives a wink of the eye as he says it? Actions do speak louder than words. Our bodies "wink" in more ways than with the eyes.

The TV has added a helpful term to the speaker's vocabulary by calling people *viewers* rather than simply *listeners.* People judge by looking, perhaps more than they do by listening. That is why speakers must learn to think in terms of the visual as well as auditory side of the speaking situation. Delivery by body aids or hinders just as all other factors in the speaking situation do. There is no in between. The body is there. It cannot be avoided in the speaking situation unless one speaks by means of radio or a tape recording. How the body is used, misused or fails to be used will have much to do with the speaker's effectiveness.

Bodily delivery is the language of emotion. Delivery is to emotion what language is to thought. You recognize this every time you walk up to a friend who hasn't opened his mouth and ask him, "Why so glum, chum?" As we say, it is "written all over his face"; i.e., he is expressing emotion by his body.

THE WHOLE BODY IS INVOLVED

A good baseball pitcher doesn't deliver the ball with his arm alone. He uses his whole body. The speaker, to be effective, must do likewise. Preaching that does not affect the *whole man* (who preaches) is not likely to affect the audience either. But first, let us turn to the more superficial side of delivery.

The appearance is the first thing that an audience sees. Often viewers judge too quickly and superficially, but, as a matter of fact, they do judge from what they see and are influenced immediately by it. Is the speaker neat, clean, well-groomed? Does he walk with a certain amount of zest and confidence? Does he really care about himself, about his cause, about his audience? The appearance provides a preliminary answer to those questions.

Poise and posture, like every other movement, have meaning. How one walks to the pulpit, confidently, hesitantly, joyously, with a spring in his step, or otherwise, speaks volumes. How does he sit: does he fidget, is he calm, is he responsive to other speakers, is he preoccupied, is he thumbing through his Bible looking for a text? All of these bodily actions betray one's emotions. They often tell whether a speaker is impatient, fearful, or nervous. Weight shifting, swaying, arm-swinging, hand-hiding, toe-teetering, and clothes-adjusting all communicate. Look at the preacher who grasps the pulpit in a death-like grip, or the one who stiff-arms it. Look at the slouch who drapes himself over the pulpit, or the one who freezes and stiffens behind it. All of these stances tell an audience, consciously or unconsciously, a great deal about the man and his attitude toward himself and his subject. They are all of importance, therefore, because they communicate, sometimes more than the words he uses and the voice that produces those words. Speakers need an alert, on-the-top-of-it posture which has flexibility and freedom and yet is poised for action. The body should suggest an attitude of humble confidence.

ACTION AND MEANING

When he moves, the speaker's movement should communicate something. All action should have helpful significance. Stepping to either side of the pulpit, for instance, should not be purposeless action, but should help the speaker say something. All action, as a rule, ought to be purposeful action. There ought to be no random movements that have no meaning to them. If one steps to either side of the pulpit, he might do so at a time when he wishes to indicate transition to a new point or change of thought. When he comes forward or leans forward in a more intimate, warmer fashion, a speaker may be indicating informality or concern, or perhaps that he is taking the audience into his confidence. Stepping backward might be used to indicate a certain remoteness to an idea, objectivity, relaxation, or that there is a clear difference of viewpoint between the speaker and his audience. But when a speaker is not aware of the meaning of such motion and never stops to interpret what he is communicating by it, he is likely to say things with his body that he never intended to say. He may actually be contradicting his message by his motions.

FACE, EYES, MOUTH

Facial expressions are quite expressive; in fact, many persons think they are the most important elements in bodily delivery. This holds true especially when speaking over television or where the speaker is in some other way brought very close to the audience. Good delivery growing out of reliving content will usually help the speaker to make the proper use of his face and mouth. But a word or two must be directed to the problem of maintaining eye contact, since this raises a special problem in bodily delivery.

Eye contact should be maintained and distributed during a speech. The false idea that one should pick out a friendly face and speak to him (or to two or three friendly faces) needs to be contradicted immediately. Do not focus directly on one or even several specified persons, but gradually let your eyes survey all. You do not want those people to feel especially privileged (or warned) and the rest to feel avoided. Everyone should feel as if you were speaking to him a reasonable proportion of the time. Eye contact conveys honesty, directness, warmth, good will and interest toward the audience. When you look at people instead of out of the window or at the ceiling or toward the floor or down at notes, you let the audience know that what you are saying is for *them*. You are not speaking for the sake of yourself or the sake of the sermon, or for the sake of the building, but you are speaking to *them*. Learn how to use notes effectively. If notes are a problem because they interfere with eye contact, learn to use less notes or become more familiar with them beforehand. But at all costs avoid the henpecking shenanigans that result from too frequent reference to notes.

GESTURES

As important as facial expressions may be, for the preacher, probably the one most important part of bodily action is the use of gestures. Good preaching demands their use. Gestures may be either overt or covert. In general, extremes should be avoided. Neither the wooden soldier nor the windmill in a tornado is to be emulated. Preachers must use both overt and covert gestures; the use of the two types is not to be thought of as an either/or matter. Such an antithesis is entirely false. The subject, the occasion, the size of the audience, the size of the auditorium, and a host of other factors must govern whether overt or covert gestures are appropriate. Every man must become expert in the use of both. At a funeral, or young people's scavenger hunt, or speaking to a YMCA board luncheon, or a Sunday morning congregation, one's gestures probably will be and ought to be distinguishable. Preaching from Matthew 23 will require gestures quite different from those used when speaking from John 14.

It might be helpful also to distinguish (as a key) between the *actor's* gestures, which in general are *imitative,* and the *speaker's* gestures, which are normally *suggestive.* When a preacher speaks, for example, of pouring water, he may give a suggestion of the act by a motion of the hand, but ordinarily he will not actually raise one hand as though holding the glass and the other as though pouring out of a pitcher into it.

There are three basic functional types of gestures. First is the *descriptive* gesture, which goes with words like, "It was *this* tall," or "The fish was *this* long." Secondly there are *emphatic* gestures which accompany words like *"No!" "Now!"* or *"Oh yeah?"* Then there are *indicative* gestures that assist phrases like, *"That* one over there," or "He went *that* way."

IMPROVING BODILY ACTION

The speaker's goal is to learn the use of free, natural and appropriate action that will aid oral communication. The word *natural* needs to be understood. It does not mean biologically natural. Naturalness in speaking is not hereditary; "natural" speech is natural because it has become *second* nature. It is actually habitual speech appropriate to content.[1] This speech comes naturally as one learns to drive a car without thinking about each action, or as he buttons his shirt without deciding whether to begin at the bottom or top. Bodily action is learned. It is cultural. The Chinese express sur-

---

[1]See Jay Adams, *op. cit.,* pp. 164 ff.

prise by sticking out the tongue, disappointment by clapping hands, and happiness by scratching ears.[2] These bodily actions are not "natural" to us, but are perfectly natural to them because that is the way they learned to express their emotions.

Practice in improving bodily action should take place in normal life situations (don't practice when speaking formally, nor should you learn specific gestures for specific speeches). Build new gestures into your repertoire, not merely into one speech. Secondly, observe natural bodily movements that you already use in animated conversation. That is, become aware of the gestures that are already natural when speaking effectively, and practice using these more often. Thirdly, because gestures should grow from feeling, and should not be planned as such, you must learn to relive the circumstances of the situation you are describing. I have already spoken about this at length in Chapter Two. Fourthly, you should learn to eliminate all bodily actions that have no purpose or meaning and, therefore, that distract. Mannerisms, such as jingling coins or keys in a pocket, buttoning and unbuttoning a coat, must be eliminated. If the habit is continued, it will not be long before the boys in the back row will begin to make book on how many times in a given sermon the mannerisms will occur. Fifthly, effeminate hand gestures and bodily actions must be replaced by masculine ones.

In order to study delivery, go to the artists and don't omit the cartoonist who has learned to exaggerate bodily actions in order to convey meaning. Until recently, there were few ways of studying bodily action in isolation. One could wear ear plugs and go to speeches, of course. (A deaf man, after Henry Clay spoke, once said, "I didn't hear a word he said, but didn't he make the motions!?") But now all that you need to do is to turn down the sound on the TV set. You may watch bodily action in this way to your heart's content.

---

[2]Clifford T. Morgan, *Introduction to Psychology*, McGraw-Hill Book Company, 1956: p. 94.

You will probably be surprised at how much content and feeling are conveyed through bodily action itself. I strongly recommend the practice.

TENSION AND FEAR (STAGE FRIGHT)

Tension is often the key problem that a beginning speaker must overcome. Sometimes he speaks of butterflies in the stomach, stage fright or clammy hands. But nervousness, as someone has said, is the penalty that we pay for being race horses rather than cows. Tension is a normal anticipation reaction before a long-awaited trip, a sports event, and a test. Some have called such excitement the original emotion.[3] Tension has been noted in a child as early as the second week. It would seem that it cannot be avoided. Four thousand combat airmen in World War II were quizzed about their feelings prior to a flight. The result of that study showed symptoms that are strikingly similar to those commonly reported during stage fright. In the order of their frequency, here are the top six: (1) a pounding heart; (2) muscular tension; (3) easily irritated, angry or sore; (4) dryness of mouth; (5) perspiration; (6) butterflies in stomach.

What actually happens in stage fright? A normal bodily state of anticipation or tension may be all that is necessary to start a vicious circle that will make one incapable of speaking well. The normal bodily state of anticipation arouses feelings in the body that may be misunderstood and thereby cause fear, which, in turn, causes the body to grow more tense, which creates more pronounced feelings, which again may be misinterpreted and bring about more fear, ad infinitum. In tension situations, the body, by psychological impetus, prepares itself for an emergency. Wise speakers know this and they know also that it is good and necessary for the body to be so prepared for speaking. They know that good speak-

---

[3]Floyd L. Ruch, *Psychology and Life,* Scott, Foresman and Company, 1948, p. 411.

ing is dependent upon bodily alertness, so they harness the tension for service. Tension often helps ideas to jell during delivery. The best sermons are those in which the jelling factor is prominent. If they jell earlier in the study they may lose some of the fire that they might otherwise have at the moment of delivery.

In an emotionally tense anticipation situation, the mind reflecting on the task ahead telegraphs the various parts of the body to prepare to the fullest, and the body mobilizes its resources. That is what the speaker needs: a body fully prepared. In relaxed situations the sympathetic system operates. Its function is to build up and conserve bodily supplies. But, when the parasympathetic system is called into service, the breathing rate, the heartbeat, circulation and other physiological functions respond appropriately. The adrenal glands (adrenal means on top of the kidneys) secrete adrenalin hormone into the blood. This hormone circulates throughout the body and affects many organs. People in stress have found themselves capable of performing tasks that they are unable to do normally. Adrenalin is a kind of supercharger that soups up the body for action. For example, a man carried a safe across the room and threw it out of the window during a fire. After the fire was over, he was asked how he did this and attempted a repeat performance. He found that in a normal state of tension he could hardly budge the safe.[4] When adrenalin reaches the liver, it helps release sugar into the blood to make more energy available for the brain and the muscles. It also speeds the heartbeat so that the blood can carry on its functions more rapidly. It converts sugar resources into sugar to be utilized more rapidly by the skeletal muscles. As the body diverts blood from the digestive system to exterior muscles, the peristaltic movements of the stomach and intestines (those warm, comfortable ripples that move our food along during the

---

[4]Ruch, *op. cit.*, p. 166.

more relaxed state of the body) stop and thereby cause the butterfly feeling. The mouth may dry up, the hair may stand on end, and the hands may feel clammy.

Tension cannot be avoided, need not be feared, but must be understood. Tension is bodily preparation, the way God has made us to enable us to meet emergencies and difficult situations. Tension makes us alert. Speakers should not seek the reduction of tension, but only of the kind of excessive tension that spirals out of control because of fear. Fear can usually be avoided by understanding the beneficial function of tension and thus brought under control of content. This means that tension, to be used properly by a speaker, must be controlled so that it varies with the variety of subject matter. Content controls the amount of tension and makes it appropriate to itself at each point. Tension problems, then, are fundamentally a matter of degree.

TENSION: A MATTER OF DEGREE

So long as tension is the speaker's servant, tension is good. In order to preach well or speak well in any circumstance one must be alert, not overly relaxed, not overly tense. A certain amount of normal tension is necessary for this alertness. Normal keying up is good because it helps, but whatever hinders is abnormal and must be dealt with. Understanding is the first of several factors that may be brought into play. The first step in learning to use tension as a servant is coming to understand its purpose and its function. That's why we have been taking the time to explain the psychosomatic effects of anticipation. When lack of understanding is the source of the problem, the fear of the unknown and the resulting undisciplined tension will disappear. When a speaker feels the butterflies in his stomach, feels his muscles tense, and has a feeling of apprehension, and understands why, he will not fear these normal feelings and thus escalate tension to an abnormal level.

But after a speaker acquires a thorough understanding of

the normal bodily sensations, if stage fright persists, there may be another problem. His difficulty may stem from pride or possibly from cowardice and guilt. Possibly he is afraid of the audience's response. Fear of this sort boils down ultimately to undue personal self concern. Assuming that his preparation is adequate, that he has spoken frequently enough to become acquainted with the speaking situation, and that he understands the dynamics of normal keying up or tension, if stage fright still persists, the speaker must plainly ask himself: "Am I afraid of my audience?" He may be concerned about his appearance. A speaker's appearance becomes an object of scrutiny, and perhaps he is concerned about audience response to it. Or, more likely, he may be concerned about audience response to his performance. Or, he may be concerned about audience response to his ideas, particularly about the response of those who disagree with him. He may fear the subsequent consequences of what he has to say. Or he may feel guilty for having failed to say what he knows God wants him to say. In that case, his anticipation is about committing the sin of cowardice. Each of these possibilities notes that a shift has occurred in the speaker's thinking. Instead of thinking of the welfare of the audience, rather than thinking about being faithful to God, he has started to think about himself. The subject matter that he wishes his audience to believe has become secondary to self concern. When a speaker begins to think, "How do I look? How am I speaking? How am I going across?" he has opened the door to the possibility of a bad case of stage fright. There is only one cure for this malady— straightening out these matters with God before preaching. The speaking situation must be put into the hands of God so that when actually preaching the speaker is lost in his subject and his concern for the audience. If one is rightly concentrating on the subject matter, he has no time to think about himself. Such thought is diversionary, it hinders concentration on the subject matter and it, therefore, hurts good speaking.

SUGGESTED PROJECTS
For Classroom or Study

In Classroom or Study

1. Ask yourself, "What do I look like as a speaker? Write a personal profile in a paragraph or two. Then ask two or three other persons who are in a position to observe you as a speaker to do the same, and compare your conclusions with theirs. What did you learn?

2. The next time you speak, ask your wife or a friend to list all mannerisms that were detected, to count the times you used verbal pauses, and to look for meaningless, distracting or awkward movements.

3. How is your eye contact? What can you do about it?

4. How does your personality affect your bodily delivery? Is personality an excuse for poor habits of delivery? Read Adams, *Competent to Counsel,* pp. 74-77, and see if you agree that personality changes can be made.

5. If stage fright is your problem, decide whether it arises from
   a. unfamiliarity with speaking. *Remedy:* take every opportunity to speak;
   b. lack of preparation. *Remedy:* prepare adequately and practice before speaking;
   c. fear of anticipation reactions due to lack of understanding. *Remedy:* read the chapter again;
   d. fear of the audience. *Remedy:* repent and speak the truth in love at any cost.

CONCLUSION

You have worked your way through a pre-preaching course in pulpit speech. In it we have not discussed homiletics, the preparation and delivery of sermons or exegesis as such. The focus has been upon speech, but always speech as it pertains to preaching. Obviously a dichotomy of this sort cannot and should not be maintained successfully at all points, so frequently homiletical matters have been handled *briefly*. The form and content of the material in this textbook presuppose the need for another course and for another text that bears directly upon the principles and practices of homiletics.

If you have worked diligently throughout this course, you should be prepared to progress to the study and practice of homiletics. If, for some reason, you do not believe you are ready, now is the time to say so. In such a case, you should make an appointment with your instructor immediately to discuss this matter.

If, on the other hand, you are ready to move ahead, let me give you one final piece of advice: don't forget the things that you have learned in this course. Homiletics is bound up so tightly with speech that, although you may not be taught these principles again, they will be presupposed in all subsequent courses. Therefore, retain this book and refer to it from time to time as you may have need. May God so use your work that the words of your mouth may be acceptable in his sight.

GENERAL INDEX

INDEX OF NAMES

168